HEALTH

Mildred Blaxter

polity

First published in 2004 by Polity Press.

Polity Press
65 Bridge Street
Cambridge CB2 1UR, UK

Polity Press
350 Main Street
Malden, MA 02148, USA

A catalogue record for this book is available from the British Library.

Library of Congress Cataloging-in-Publication Data
Blaxter, Mildred.
Health / Mildred Blaxter.
    p. ; cm. – (Key concepts)

Includes bibliographical references and index.   ISBN 0-7456-3082-0
(hb : alk. paper) – ISBN 0-7456-3083-9 (pb : alk. paper)
1. Social medicine.   2. Health.

[DNLM: 1. Health. WA 100 B645h 2004]   I. Title.   II. Key concepts
(Polity Press)
RA418.B5745 2004
306.4′61–dc21

                                                                    2003012590

Typeset in 10.5 on 12 pt Sabon
by SNP Best-set Typesetter Ltd., Hong Kong
Printed and bound in Great Britain by MPG Books, Bodmin, Cornwall

For further information on Polity, visit our website: www.polity.co.uk

Health

KEY CONCEPTS

Published

Contents

Introduction

I don't think I know when I am healthy, I only know if I am ill.

office worker aged twenty-eight; Blaxter 1990

My health is a reflection of my lifestyle – I need to be spiritually, mentally, emotionally and physically whole to be truly healthy. I believe complete wholeness is only attainable through reconciliation with God.

herbalist; Stainton Rogers 1991

Q: Are men healthier than women or are women healthier than men?
A: I think men are on the whole healthier than women due to the fact that I think they feel better. I think they feel healthier. They may have the same aches and pains, but if a man doesn't notice it, or doesn't want to notice it, I would tend to think that's healthier. The woman may live longer because she does notice it and maybe takes care of it, but if he feels better, who is healthier? It gets back to what my interpretation of being healthy is: if you feel healthy, you are healthy. Now a doctor may have a different interpretation than that. You have a foreign body invading your system, he would say you are not healthy. And from this reality he is right. But not from my reality . . . if I feel healthy, I'm healthy. If I feel sick, I'm sick.

Crawford 1984

Health is to feel proud – when you can go out and you can hold your head up, look good. You don't have so many hang-ups, and you think straight.

computer operator, twenty-five; Blaxter 1990

Health is being able to walk around better and doing some work in the house when my knees let me.

woman of seventy-nine; Blaxter 1990

. . . illness is a kind of rest, when you can be free of your every-day burdens . . . For me, illness is breaking off from social life, from life outside and social obligations.

Herzlich 1973

What is health? That's a silly question!

driver of thirty-nine; Blaxter 1990

What is health? Many studies have asked ordinary people this question, and their replies, as these brief examples from research studies in the USA, the UK and France show, range from the thoughtful to the dismissive. Few people think about their health all of the time, but for most it is, at least inter-mittently, an important topic. How are you? The common greeting may not actually expect an answer in medical terms, but health is one of the most ubiquitous topics of conversa-tion in everyday life. At the same time, health and medicine are major sections of the social organization of any society: a great deal of resources and manpower go into systems for the promotion of health and the management of disease.

It may seem obvious that we must know what 'health' is. However, it is not only something on which individuals can have very different views, but also a concept which has inspired endless theorizing and dispute throughout the centuries.

This volume attempts to summarize where we are now, in the early twenty-first century, in thinking about health. The emphasis is on contemporary ideas and their development during the last century or so, including speculation about where they are now leading. However, the traces of long past systems and beliefs will always be relevant. Similarly, the emphasis is upon what is known as 'Western scientific medicine', because this is the system to which most developed societies ascribe and which developing societies tend to adopt. This is not, though, to denigrate other, non-Western, systems of belief, or to ignore the way in which 'alternative' ideas are incorporated into modern ideas of health. The central discipline here is medical sociology. But others make contributions – psychology, biological science, clinical medicine, social epidemiology, philosophy, anthropology, history of medicine, policy and politics. This, again, shows how deeply embedded ideas about health are, and how many perspectives may be brought to bear.

The volume is not presented as a textbook, but as an introduction to *ideas* about health and illness which may provide students of any of these disciplines, or those in the health professions, with provocative ways of thinking about the concepts. Besides its intellectual interest, this has an essentially practical purpose. As will become evident, ways of defining health have always influenced the practice of healers and the organization of care, and continue to play a part in determining the social policies of nations. The meaning of health is neither simple nor unchanging.

1

How is Health Defined?

Health may be defined differently by doctors and their patients, and over time and place. One of the most pervasive definitions, though, is simply normality, with illness as a deviation from the normal. The definition of disease as abnormality or damage – physiological, biochemical or psychological – held sway in modern thought for most of the last century. It is represented in lay thought by the replies commonly given in surveys to an invitation to define health: health is not being ill, health is having no disease. It is represented in clinical medicine by the whole array of tests and standards, rapidly growing in sophistication, to measure 'normal' body size and weight, blood composition, lung capacity, functioning of the liver, and so on.

This definition raises many problems, however. What is normal – normal for what, and for whom? (Clinical standards usually assume for a particular age and gender, but no more.) 'Normal' can have many meanings: average, most representative, the most common value, central in a distribution, habitual or optimal. Are we talking about the average for a given population, or some ideal? The 'perfect' is not only impossible of attainment, but also not necessarily to be desired. As Hippocrates noted in the *Aphorisms*:

> In athletics a perfect condition that is at its highest pitch is treacherous. Such conditions cannot stay the same or remain

at rest, and, change for the better being impossible, the only possible change is for the worse.

On the other hand, normal defined as average may not mean perfectly healthy, and the average – consider the examples of body weight or cholesterol level – may not be at all what clinicians regard as the 'norm' or ideal to be aimed for. What is normal degeneration in old age: are all the old unhealthy? Not all deviations from the normal are to be deplored or 'treated': some can be positively beneficial, and others are irrelevant to health. Erde (1979: 36) noted:

> If you are 80 or running a marathon, what is normal would differ from the 'norm' of someone age 20 or asleep. Furthermore, if you can run two marathons and no one else can, you may be abnormal and yet as healthy as can be. If your I.Q. is 100 it is normal. If it is 140, your mind's functions are not in a normal state. We need to know what 'normal' means, before we can tell whether someone has it or is it.

In other words, normal can be descriptive or proscriptive, and if it is proscriptive it has to depend on the state of knowledge or accepted current theory. A softer version is the recognition that there is a great range of normal variability, and only that which falls outside it need be considered as ill health. The range has still to be defined, perhaps arbitrarily.

Health as the absence of illness

For a time in the mid-twentieth century there was promulgation of the idea of disease or ill health as those phenomena which deviate from the norm in such a way as to place the individual at biological disadvantage. The healthy are those who are not biologically disadvantaged. To some extent this avoids the problems of the definition of normality, since those deviations which have no consequences are irrelevant. But it created new problems in the definition of disadvantage, which was usually described very specifically as shortened life and reduced fertility.

Commentators in the field of mental health used this to argue opposed positions: though no physiological abnormalities had so far been found to account for a condition such as schizophrenia, nevertheless it *was* a disease, using the biological disadvantage criteria. On the other hand, it was pointed out that many forms of mental ill health did not reduce life expectancy or fertility: was it impossible to call them diseases? In general, the focus on length of life and fertility seemed too Darwinian (disease is anything which interferes with the preservation of the species) and too restrictive.

Normal illness

A more subjective view can be taken, of course, resting the definition of health not on measurable, clinically defined abnormality, but on people's own perception of the experience of symptoms or feelings of illness. The problem is that the norm becomes even more difficult to define. It is commonly demonstrated in studies of populations that to experience no symptoms of ill health at all – never to have pain, mild dysfunction, infection or injury – is in fact highly abnormal: most of us, most of the time, can identify something which we might call a symptom of an illness. Only a small proportion of this is taken for professional attention and diagnosis as disease, and much of it is self-limiting.

Any definition of health as the absence of self-perceived illness has to deal with the fact that this perception varies widely among individuals and depends on situations. Questions have again to be raised about normal illness – normal for this particular person, normal for this sort of individual, normal in these circumstances? – with even less certainty about what the average is, or what would be considered as the ideal.

Disease as deviance

The idea of health as the absence of disease or illness, and disease as deviation from the norm, elides easily into ill health seen as 'deviance' from social or moral norms. The objective observation of a lack of 'normality' meets a very ancient and universal tendency to see the sick person as in some way morally tainted, bewitched, possibly responsible for their own misfortunes, and at best being offered the opportunity to show some strength of character in suffering. Ill health usually has negative connotations: it is 'bad luck' for the individual whose life it disturbs. Ill health also harms the functioning or the prosperity of the society in which they live: the sick are not productive, they may require resources, and they must be controlled and monitored. Thus the American sociologist Talcott Parsons's treatment of sickness as a role designed to allow 'deviants' to find conditional and provisional legitimacy was influential in early medical sociology.

Health as balance or homeostasis

A link between the concepts of health and normality lies in the ancient idea of homeostasis – the idea that the normal state of the body is order, and its systems are designed to be self-righting. This old idea was given new life when it was realized that not only a pathogen, but also a host – the body which was being invaded or harmed – was actively involved in the development of ill health. When a system was being attacked by a specific agent, or was disordered by biological error or stresses and accidents in the environment, regulatory mechanisms came into play. Restoring the normal involves not only equilibrium of the human organism – mind and body – with its environment, but also internal equilibrium within the body's functions and organs. Ill health arises when the balance is disturbed. In modern times this approach gained attraction from its association with the growth of ecology as a natural science.

As commentators such as Mishler (1981) have pointed out, this has elements of older, perhaps less scientific concepts. It echoes the classical Platonic model of health as harmony among the body's processes and systems, and disease as a state of discord, and the Galenian concept of disease as a disturbance of function. Before the rise of modern medicine, not only the cultures of the West but all the great cultures of the world, such as those of China or India, held that health is to be defined as the right balance between supernatural beings, the environment, and processes within the body. Disease as imbalance had to be corrected by the remedying of deficiency (by, for instance, diet) or the removal of excess (by, for instance, purging or bleeding).

A theory of health has to accommodate the fact that all living things have some ability to respond to changing environments. The accepted explanation is that the environment does not wholly determine the properties of the organism which is, at least partly, self-organized and capable of change. Modern medicine shows that in certain physiological aspects the body is a homeostatic machine: for instance, the immune system responds when infection enters the system, and loss of blood by injury is responded to by vasoconstriction to keep blood pressure steady. The capacity to sustain equilibrium, or more generally the ability of the body to heal itself, can be regarded as a measure of its healthiness. These ideas, ancient in principle, are elaborated by the most modern science. As a total model of health, however, homeostasis has limitations. This is undoubtedly part of healthiness, but some healthy functions – reproduction, for instance – upset equilibrium rather than maintain it, and not all systems are even theoretically self-righting. It can be accepted that some aspects of equilibrium are crucial to life, without confusing the idea of homeostasis with the broader ideal of the normal.

Health as function

This does, however, move away a little from the essentially negative definitions. Another, and even more positive, way is in terms of function. The elderly person quoted on p. 1 expressed this: health is being able to do things. Functional health can be thought of in terms of having a fit body, not being restricted in any way, being able to do the things one wants or needs to do, all the natural functions of ordinary life being performed freely and without pain. This, again, connects to modern ecological ideas by being defined as being well adapted to the environment, engaging in effective inter-

action with the physical and social world. Ill health is incapacity, whether caused by disease, accident, the degeneration
of old age, or less than perfectly functional development at
the start of life. Disease is failure in adaptation, and is dysfunctional both to individuals themselves and to the societies
of which they are a part.

Another popular functional definition of health is as 'the
ability to reach desired goals' (Porn 1993), essentially a
concept in terms of adaptive functioning. There are some
obvious problems with this definition of health. As Erde
(1979: 35) commented: 'Being stuck in a door would auto-
matically make someone unhealthy if this definition were
held.' The difficulty is partly the obvious relativity: it depends
on what one wants or needs to do. It depends on the requirements of the individual or the situation: perfect function in a
young athlete and in an elderly, sedentary person represents
different physical capacities.

Health as function easily elides into health as fitness, with
the question 'fitness for what?' unanswered. A very restricted
answer is simply 'the activities of daily living' – mobility,
caring for oneself, working. This immediately tends to define
those with physical, sensory or mental disabilities as unfit and
raises questions about whether impairments – inability to see
or hear, for instance – are to be called ill health. Those who
speak for people with disabilities would contest this fiercely,
arguing that any impairment is more or less disabling depending on the environment: there are disabling environments, not
disabled people.

Health as state or status

Confusion commonly arises because of another problem: is
health to be defined as a temporary state (am I ill today?) or
a longer-term status (am I basically a healthy or unhealthy
person?)? That people themselves clearly make this distinction is attested to by replies to polite questions such as 'How
are you?', which are often 'Well, I have a cold, but in general
I'm very healthy', or answers in health surveys to questions
such as 'Are you in good/fair/poor health?', which can take

difficult-to-categorize forms such as 'I've got diabetes, but my health is excellent.'

The distinction is not entirely the one which medicine conventionally adopts between the acute and the chronic. All ill health cannot be forced into one of these two categories: people may be 'chronic' sufferers from acute conditions, long-term chronic disease results in varying degrees of acute illness at any particular time. 'State' represents the present health state of the individual, distinct from (though of course commonly associated with) their health status, or the general characteristic of being healthy or unhealthy. Health 'status' is a longer-term attribute, changing rapidly only in the event of the sudden and unexpected onset of serious illness or permanently damaging trauma. Health state, on the other hand, is an erratic condition, relevant to health status only if it derives from it or if (because of its typicality or frequency) it reflects back to be incorporated into health status.

Health state and health status have some association with the health economist's concept of health as 'stock' or capital and health as 'flow'. Health capital (a concept discussed in a later chapter) can be conceived of as the cumulation of health states – illnesses, accidents, malfunctions, increases or decreases in fitness – which the individual or the group experiences.

The biomedical model

There are thus many ways in which health might be defined, for the most part resting on ideas of the 'normal' and of seeing health as opposed to disease or illness. In practice, the definition of health has always been the territory of those who define its opposite: healers, or practitioness of medicine as a science or a body of practical knowledge. Since medicine is one of society's major systems, it is obvious that it is these definitions which will be institutionalized and embodied in law and administration, though the extent to which 'lay' models add to or diverge from this body of ideas will be considered later.

The basic paradigm of medicine since the development of the germ theory in the nineteenth century has been what is called the biomedical model. In its stereotypical form, this has been based on, and almost wholly dominated by, the methods and principles of the biological sciences. It would be natural for such a model to be based on the 'disease' which it is the function of medicine to treat, and thus on ill health rather than health.

Historians of medicine note how two ways of thinking about health have appeared and disappeared throughout the development of Western medical practice. Disease can be seen as independent of the patient:

> The doctor will be different in the Western tradition, because he will be looking *through* the ill person to the disease that caused the illness. The trained doctor will have a form of con-tract, not with individuals, but with the diseases that use these individuals as media. (Neve 1995: 479)

Alternatively, as in Hippocratic medicine, the individual, with all his or her particular circumstances, diet, dreams and habits, can be seen as of first importance.

The first way came to predominate after the Enligh-tenment, when the work of scientists such as Pasteur and Koch in the nineteenth century demonstrated that specific diseases could be introduced into the body by specific micro-organisms. The earlier 'anatomists' and pathologists had begun to trace out the structures of the body and the way it functioned, introducing mechanistic models of the processes involved. The new bacteriological science now, however, transformed notions of the practice of medicine. It meant that doctors need no longer be limited by their observation of mechanical processes or rely on accounts of subjective symp-toms. Science, and the body's own immune system, could conquer the ancient scourges of cholera, diphtheria or tuber-culosis by vaccination and inoculation.

The fundamental principles of the biomedical model began to include the following.

(1)   The first principle is what is called the *doctrine of spe-cific etiology*, that is, the idea that all disease is caused by the-oretically identifiable agents such as germs, bacteria or parasites. The influence of germ theory was powerful, spread-ing rapidly from infectious diseases to others produced by

known, specific, causes – metabolic processes, disturbances of growth or function. An obvious corollary of such a model is that explanation will be thought to be 'better' – more complete – the more that description has moved from an initial taxonomy, or categorization, of individual symptoms through the identification of a 'syndrome' or cluster of symptoms to a final diagnosis of a disease with a single cause.

Criticisms of this principle focused principally on the suggestion that it oversimplified biological processes now known to be very complex. For many diseases there are multiple and interacting causes. Moreover, such a principle looks only to the agent of disease, and ignores the host, and the possibilities of biological adaptation. The scientist and medical historian Rene Dubos, in his influential books *Mirage of Health* and *Man Adapting* nearly half a century ago, asked, for instance, why does infection not *always* produce disease? Why is disease rare though infectious agents are present everywhere? The principle is much more easily applicable to acute conditions than to chronic ill health and is difficult to apply to mental disorders.

(2)   A second principle of the biomedical model is called the *assumption of generic disease* – the idea that each disease has its own distinguishing features that are universal, at least within the human species. These will be the same in different cultures and at different times, unless the disease-producing agent itself changes. As Sydenham declared in the seventeenth century: 'All diseases should be reduced to certain definite species with the same care which we see exhibited by botanists in their description of plants.'

Criticisms of this focus on the rather obvious point that diseases are differently defined in different cultures and that medical definitions of disease have clearly changed over time. Each new advance in knowledge of physiology and each new wave of technology has added new definitions of ill health to the accepted canon. Despite the doctrine of specific etiology, many conditions which are still only symptoms or syndromes are recognized within medicine as 'diseases'. More generally, it can easily be shown (chapter 2) that what is viewed as illness in any particular society and at any historical time depends on cultural norms and social values.

It has been argued that in practice a condition is defined by medicine as a disease if and when it is felt that clinical means are appropriate for treating it: ill health is simply what doctors treat. The answer that doctors give to the question 'Is this a disease?' is really an answer to the question 'Can I, or do I want to, treat this person?' (Linder 1965). This is not always true, of course, for doctors treat many people they do not see as 'diseased'. But it can be demonstrated that frequently the act of diagnosis is primarily the process of deciding what the appropriate treatment is (Blaxter 1978).

Thus 'new' diagnoses – new diseases – such as alcoholism, post-traumatic stress disorder, chronic fatigue syndrome, are born through an interaction of new knowledge about both their possible causes and how they might possibly be helped. As a definition of disease, 'what doctors treat' has obvious problems, however. It implies that no one can be ill until recognized as such, and leaves the concept at the mercy of idiosyncratic individual medical decisions.

(3) A third principle of scientific biomedicine is that it accepts the model of all ill health as *deviation from the normal*, especially the normal range of measurable biological variables. In the mid-nineteenth century Virchow proclaimed that disease was simply altered physiology: 'Nothing but life under altered conditions.' There is an association with the definition of health as equilibrium and disease as a disturbance of the body's functions, with the purpose of medical technology the restoration to equilibrium. The immune, or endocrine, or neuropsychological, systems attempt to restore the 'normal', and the purpose of medicine is to instigate or assist this process. But medical science now realizes that the human organism has no set pattern for structure and function, and it is often unclear where normal variation ends and abnormality begins. Kendall (1975: 305) asked: 'Is hypertension a disease, and if so what is the level beyond which the blood pressure is abnormal?', and suggested that it was in fact this example of hypertension which finally discredited the nineteenth-century assumption that there was always an observable, measurable distinction between illness and normal health.

(4)   The fourth postulate of medical science was that it was held to be based on the principles of *scientific neutrality*. Medicine adopts not only the rational method of science but also its values – objectivity and neutrality on the part of the observer, and the view of the human organism as simply the product of biological (and perhaps psychological) processes over which the individuals themselves have little control.

The reply to this is that the practice of medicine, whatever its theory, is always deeply embedded in the larger society. It cannot be neutral, for there are wider social, political and cultural forces dictating how it does its work and how the unhealthy are dealt with. The diagnoses of female hysteria in the nineteenth century, or Gulf War Syndrome in the twenty-first, cannot be thought to be culturally or politically neutral.

Contemporary biomedicine

Residues of all four of these postulates can be found in contemporary medical practice. But it would be a caricature to present them as defining modern medicine: it is a long time since the medical model espoused crude models of cause and effect. The advance of medical science has directed attention to necessary and sufficient rather than single causes. The assumption that every disease had a distinct cause, both necessary and sufficient, had to be given up as it became apparent that a great many interacting factors, whether inside or outside the individual body, contributed to any ill health. To regard one as *the* cause became increasingly arbitrary. During the first half of the twentieth century, for instance, it was noted that the tubercular baccillus was a necessary cause of tuberculosis – that is, the disease would not be present if the agent was absent – but it was not a *sufficient* cause. The baccillus was widespread in many populations, but only a minority of people actually developed the disease.

The model of the causation of ill health changed, for example, in the instance of 'flu', from:

Biomedicine now admits multiple and interactive causes, and that the whole may be more than simply the sum of the parts. The rise of psychology was also relevant in altering the

invasion of virus → symptom (sore throat, fever, etc.)
to:
invasion of virus → response of immune system → symptom
and eventually to:

$$
\left.\begin{array}{l}
\text{status of immune} \\
\quad \text{system} \\
\text{and} \\
\text{response of} \\
\quad \text{antibodies} \\
\text{and} \\
\text{genetic} \\
\quad \text{susceptibility}
\end{array}\right\} \rightarrow \begin{array}{l} \text{invasion} \\ \text{of virus} \end{array} \rightarrow \begin{array}{l} \text{response of} \\ \text{physical and} \\ \text{psychological} \\ \text{systems} \end{array} \rightarrow \text{symptom}
$$

purely mechanistic model of illness. Increasingly evidence was gathered – to add sufficient scientific proof to what had prob-ably always been personally felt and professionally recog-nized – to show that psychological factors affect many illness conditions, and many if not most conditions have some psy-chosomatic elements: that is, they are genuine organic con-ditions but have at least some psychological factor in their cause.

This is, however, an elaboration of the medical model rather than a fundamental revision. Social and psychological causes of ill health – stress, unhappiness, life events – are admitted as agents of disease, or contributing factors, but they are not themselves defined as ill health.

In the light of the dates of the most influential critiques of the medical model – many decades ago – and this movement, strong in the mid-twentieth century, to include the psycho-logical within it, it would obviously be foolish to present the pure 'biomedical model' as still separate and in opposition to the 'social model' which will be considered next. Modern medicine has moved on, to incorporate elaborate ideas about the various and interrelated causes of ill health. However, though 'Koch's postulates' of specific etiology and so on may not nowadays be taught in medical schools, their echoes still sound in medical discourse and their influence can still be seen in medical practice. Studies of the way in which doctors make diagnoses demonstrate this, while at the same time lip-service is paid to the importance of the 'social'. Moreover, even when social and psychological influences are admitted, this is still a very negatively oriented approach to health.

The social model

Around the middle of the twentieth century there was increasing dissatisfaction with the dominant model of health offered by biomedicine. The preoccupation with disease and illness made it less able to deal with any positive concept of health. The ideology which viewed the individual in mechanistic ways justified ever-increasing use of medical technologies, precluding the exercise of other therapies and diminishing the importance (and the resources) allocated to positive health, or preventive medicine.

Notably, the American philosopher Ivan Illich (1974: 918) claimed that medical professional practice was itself a threat to health, identifying the syndrome he called 'medical nemesis':

> With the last decade medical professional practice has become a major threat to health. Depression, infection, disability, dysfunction, and other specific iatrogenic diseases now cause more suffering than all accidents from traffic or industry . . . By transforming pain, illness and death from a personal challenge into a technical problem, medical practice expropriates the potential of people to deal with their human condition in an autonomous way and becomes the sources of a new kind of un-health.

The ideal that the 'normal' state of the human body was defined by order and homeostasis, and the purpose of medicine was to assist or replace this process, was notably addressed by Antonovsky (1979), who offered an alternative paradigm he called 'salutogenic'. The emphasis on health as simply the absence of disease encouraged thinking about only two categories, the healthy and the diseased. Stressors and pathogens are, Antonovsky pointed out, part of the human condition, and not always 'bad' for us. Moreover, the 'mirage of health' described by Dubos (1959) is conjured up – we want to believe that science can produce a Utopia of disease-free and lengthy life. Scientists look only for their 'magic bullet'. Antonovsky (1979: 203) pointed out that this means more attention is paid to disease than to health: 'We do not ask about the smokers who do not get lung cancer, the drinkers who stay out of accidents, the Type As who do not have coronaries.'

Thinking 'salutogenically' involves turning to a focus on what facilitates health, rather than on what causes or prevents disease – a focus on successful physical and mental coping.

Thus Antonovsky developed a concept 'sense of coherence', the components of which were measures of the extent to which individuals perceived the world as comprehensible (ordered, making sense, structured, predictable, rather than disordered, random, chaotic), manageable (with the resources available) and meaningful (making emotional sense). This was found to be associated with health because those who had high measures of these qualities were more likely to cope with situations, maintain their health, and display a psychic 'resistance' somewhat like immunological resistance. The precise measurement and elaboration of this idea has perhaps been overtaken, but it was an important step towards a concept of positive health.

There was some feeling that the most angry critiques of the biomedical model were wilfully ignoring the contributions of modern science to human welfare. However, claims to the unique truth of biomedicine were weakened by some loss of faith in scientific objectivity and a distrust of a Frankenstein technology that could run out of control, and this was part of the modern movement towards a new model usually called 'social health'.

The concept of social or holistic health incorporates many differences of emphasis, though it has to be noted that it is more than simply the recognition that 'social factors' such as poverty or ways of behaving have to be included in a model of the causes of ill health. The social model is a different construction, locating biological processes within their social contexts, and considering the person as a whole rather than a series of distinct bodily systems. The medical model, in terms of specific health risks, does not encompass all of what health means to an individual. The American sociologist Irving Zola (1975: 184) memorably demonstrated this by quoting a physician speculating on what, based on current knowledge at the time, would be the composite picture of an individual with a low risk of developing coronary artery disease:

> . . . an effeminate municipal worker or embalmer completely lacking in physical or mental alertness and without drive, ambition, or competitive spirit: who has never attempted to meet a deadline of any kind; a man with poor appetite, subsisting on fruits and vegetables laced with corn and whale oil, detesting tobacco, spurning ownership of radio, television, or motorcar, with full head of hair but scrawny and unathletic appearance, yet constantly straining his puny muscles by exercise. Low in income, blood pressure, blood sugar, uric acid and cholesterol, he has been taking nicotinic acid, pyridoxine, and long term anti-coagulant therapy ever since his prophylactic castration.

Zola went on to comment:

> Nor does it really matter if instead of the above depressing picture we were guaranteed six more inches in height, thirty more years of life or drugs to expand our potentialities and potencies; we should still be able to ask, what do six inches matter, in what kind of environment will the thirty additional years be spent, or who will decide what potentialities and potencies will be expanded and what curbed?

The social model is holistic and organic rather than reductionist and mechanical. A mechanical system acts according to its programming, its instructions, or natural laws. In the medical model built on the Cartesian principle of the body as a machine, disorders can be corrected by repairing or replacing parts of the organism. Holism describes the view that the whole cannot be explained simply by the sum of the parts, just as 'healthiness' cannot be explained by a list of 'risk factors'. Every disturbance in a system involves the whole system. Human beings are living networks formed by cognitive processes, values, and purposive intentions, not simply interacting components. This complex system selects its own inputs and responds to the meanings ascribed to them.

The development of this social model has, among the public, been accompanied by a growing enthusiasm for alternative therapies, which tend to rest on holistic principles. Slowly, these too have been incorporated to some extent into the mainstream model. In particular, health is perceived as a positive state, not simply an absence of disease or an 'average' condition.

In 1948 the World Health Organization defined health as 'a state of complete physical, mental and social well-being, and not merely the absence of disease or infirmity', and this is generally held to epitomize the social model of health. There are obvious problems about this definition, which seems to incorporate the whole of human existence and has been criticized as difficult to measure and impossible to achieve. However, it does draw attention to the kind of multifaceted, holistic and socially conscious definition of health which is most favoured in contemporary Western societies. Recognizing that a sense of well-being is essentially subjective does not make it less amenable to investigation and promotion. Movements such as that known in the UK as the 'New Public Health' become relevant, and the aim becomes an attempt to change the health of societies or groups by altering their environment (making places healthier to live in) or their behaviour (health promotion to change unhealthy lifestyles).

Health, disease, illness and sickness

In summary, in the biomedical model health is obviously most easily defined by the absence of disease, though the model is also compatible with more positive definitions in terms of equilibrium or normal functioning. In the social model, health is a positive state of wholeness and well-being, associated with, but not entirely explained by, the absence of disease, illness or physical and mental impairment. The concepts of health and ill health are asymmetrical: they are not simply opposites. The absence of disease may be part of health, but health is more than the absence of disease.

But the issue remains: how do we distinguish the objective notion of disease and the more general idea of illness? It has become common in English-speaking countries to give different meanings to the words disease, illness, sickness and suffering. *Disease* is the medically defined pathology. *Illness* is the subjective experience of ill health. *Sickness* is the social role of those defined as diseased or ill: as Parsons (1951) first noted, the sick are treated differently to the well, behave in certain ways, and have different expectations required of them. There are problems about this usage, since not every language has equivalent words. But it does have value in pointing out that these three concepts are not the same. That they are different, in English at least, is nicely shown by Erde (1979: 40):

> Consider some of the differences (similarities would show us nothing – or something else) between some of the ordinary uses of two of these terms. (i) There are sick plants and sick dogs, but *no* ill plants and *no* ill dogs; (ii) there are sick days and sick leave and sick call but *no* ill of these; (iii) there is 'homesick' but *no* 'home ill'; (iv) there is 'sickening' but not 'illing'; (v) there is 'sick society' but *no* 'ill society'; (vi) there is 'ill wind' and 'ill tempered' and 'ill informed' but *no* sick of these; (vii) there is 'sick humor' and 'ill humored'.
>
> This suggests that 'ill' is a much more general word than 'sick'. 'Ill' seems to mean 'wrong' or 'violating the norms' but it applies to a much wider range of subjects than does 'sick'. Nevertheless it has a softer tone to it, it seems less harsh somehow. 'Terminal illness' is not nice, but it is nicer than 'terminal sickness' would be. 'Mental illness' is less judgmental, less accusatory than 'mentally sick'.

People may be ill, that is, feel themselves to have something wrong with them, without (known) disease. Medicine tends to call them hypochondriac if they complain too loudly, but there is more subtle appreciation nowadays that it is very possible to be ill without any – at least, so far identified – disease. Stepping into the doctor's surgery, the person with an illness is transformed into a patient with a diagnosis. Even if no illness had been perceived before, a routine test may show high blood pressure. The patient is then 'suffering' from hypertension (important as a risk factor in heart disease), and the drugs offered to treat the disease are a sign of their legitimated status as 'sick', even if only mildly so. There is some evidence that people so defined may then perceive themselves as having symptoms (as well as perhaps experiencing side effects of drugs) which they did not before – that is, being ill.

Sickness is a useful word for the role that can be assumed by the ill, though not necessarily: it is possible to feel oneself ill or be diagnosed as having disease without adopting the role of the sick person – that is, seeking medical help, assuming or seeking 'permission' to give up one's normal roles or occupations in life, expecting special consideration. People may be diseased, injured or functionally incapacitated without being ill, or without claiming to be sick. It is very common, in surveys of health, to find people with severe disabilities claiming that their health is 'excellent', or the old with many degenerative diseases saying that their health is 'marvellous'.

Both illness and disease imply the potential for suffering, though neither is defined by it. Many who are regarded as ill do not complain of suffering, either because they ignore that which might cause others to claim it, or because their illness does not involve the types of symptom (pain, disability) usually considered to be distressing.

Disease may exist without subjectively experienced symptoms, as in a silent cancer. Moreover, modern medical science produced many liminal states – states which are neither sick nor well, but mark a boundary: potentially ill, but effectively well, in remission but not cured, at known risk of disease which has not yet developed. The American social anthropologist Arthur Frank (1995: 8) described the people he suggests belong to the 'remission society':

> These people are all around, though often invisible. A man standing behind me in the airport security check announces that he has a pacemaker; suddenly his invisible 'condition' becomes an issue. Once past the metal detector, his 'remission' status disappears into the background.

Previously, he suggests, when curative medicine was wholly to the foreground, people could be well *or* sick. In postmodern times, sickness and health shade into each other:

Instead of a static picture on the page where light is separated from dark, the image is like a computer graphic where one shape is constantly in process of becoming the other.

The epigram 'disease (and trauma) is what doctors treat, illness is what patients experience' is often cited. It is superficially attractive but facile. It is true that the process of diagnosis can be seen (often) as the way in which illness is turned into disease, and doctors may try to avoid diagnosing conditions for which they, personally, feel that they have no treatment available. Illness is experienced in time, place and individuality, while disease is abstracted and generalized. Frankenberg (1992) suggests that it is a characteristic of Western medicine that doctors are required to distance themselves from the current story of this illness presented to them and translate it into timeless disease.

Nevertheless, doctors do treat illness. Individuals do subjectively perceive disease. Indeed, much of the impetus to consultation with a doctor is the patient's question 'Is this disease?' And much of treatment is the doctor's answer 'I do not know (yet) but I will treat your illness.' The suggestion that an ill health could be defined as 'that which doctors treat' can give rise to 'measures' of population health in terms of medical consultations, hospitalizations, and so on, which have their own uses but are certainly not measures of health.

How is health measured?

These complicated definitions, of people as diseased, ill or sick, as healthy or unhealthy, and of health as state or status, are woven into ordinary life and usually accommodated. Precise definitions are needed only sometimes, when administrative or organizational decisions have to be made. Should resources be spent on this treatment? Is it legitimate for this person to be away from work? Does this individual come into a category which society has decided to support? We often do want to measure general, overall 'healthiness', however, and this discussion suggests that it is not going to be as easy as we might think. The measurement of the health of populations – to describe what social or environmental influences are at work, or which groups of people or types of individual are more or less healthy – is full of pitfalls. Equally, there are difficulties for the individual wanting to know how 'healthy' they are, and for the policy-makers, service-providers and medical scientists who need to have information about the health of populations.

The many measures that are currently used reflect the issues that have been discussed. Some describe health state, and some health status. Some consider only disease, and some focus on illness. Some depend on the social role of sickness. Many rely on the idea of the 'normal' or average, but others refer to some ideal condition.

Firstly, as in national mortality statistics, there is longevity, or *life expectancy*, the chance of dying at a younger or an older age. This is usually the basic way in which nations are compared with each other or populations compared over time. It has the obvious limitation that the fact of life or death is certainly not all there is to say about health. Also, though mortality statistics can relate only to the past, and predictions from past trends can (certainly in the individual case) be no more than probabilities, the interest of the individual in life expectancy relates (of course) to the future timing of death, and the interests of policy are usually in predictions. Moreover, life expectancy is not as simple a measure as sometimes presented. Life expectancy at birth and life expectancy after the dangers of infancy have passed are very different things. As the years increase, the difference between groups tends to lessen, until eventually all are subject only to biological inevitability.

Other measures concern the existence of *disease* – necessarily, that disease which has already been identified by a medical system. Following the definition of health as some norm, it can be measured by standard tests of *physiological and psychological functioning*. These are the evidence of health that doctors are likely to apply.

Health may also be measured by the *experience of symptoms*, subjectively declared. This will relate to a definition of health as the absence of illness. That different individual people – and, more importantly, different types of people, such as men and women, the young and the old – seem to perceive symptoms differently complicates any use of this as an objective measure.

Similarly, the functional model of health appears when health is measured by the *ability to carry out normal daily activities*. An early distinction between ill, diseased and sick was made by Bauman (1961) as (a) feeling-state conceptions ('I don't feel well'), (b) clinical descriptions ('there is something wrong with my back') and (c) performance conceptions ('I am staying in bed today'). In survey methods of measuring health, Bauman pointed out that only the last, performance, is really useful, because feeling states are difficult to measure and clinical states require professional interpretation. Thus an early measure of health, the Sickness Impact Profile, was devised as an elaborated functional measure, assessing dysfunction in terms of many categories such as social interaction, work, locomotion, leisure, intellectual functioning, and others. However, ill health as restriction of activities is still most discriminatory as the 'negative' end of the scale, and selects out relatively few in most populations. There are also the problems of 'normal for whom'?

Health as *fitness* is perhaps a more positive measure which may be derived from tests of physiological functioning, considering the conditions and abilities of the individual without reference to their actual use in daily activities: that is, conventionally, principally their muscle strength, lung capacity, cardiac fitness, and so on. This is, again, a rather restricted definition of total health, but has at least the advantage of offering a continuous scale which can run from the least fit to the extremely fit, rather than the dichotomous definitions of with/without disease, able/unable, or ill/not ill.

Often, the health of populations is 'measured' simply by asking people to assess it themselves. While this is a surprisingly useful measure, in that it does seem to distinguish quite clearly the medically defined healthy or unhealthy, the problem of how people decide to categorize their own health adds layers of complication. Which of all the definitions that have been discussed are they including, with what relative weights?

Finally, and sometimes as a measure of despair, health is assessed simply as whether people have had contact with a medical system or have been unable to work because of sickness. The problems of interpreting these as 'real' measures of health are obvious. A conceptual base and associated measures are lacking for positive health. Indicators therefore tend to be distributed towards the 'unhealthy' end of the continuum. These ways of measuring health are also difficult to combine. Is it 'better' to feel well-balanced and happy, even in the presence of disease, or to be without illness but poorly adapted to one's environment? Is the athlete with disabilities healthy or not? How different is the meaning of health in youth and in old age? Measures that describe an individual's health state or status, or characterize the health of populations, have to focus on the different purposes for which these descriptions might be required. To some degree, measures acquire popularity depending on the predominant disease patterns of an era. Communicable diseases and infections lend themselves to population measures of morbidity and mortality. As chronic and degenerative diseases become more important, functional definitions and measures of disability come to the fore. The broad definition of social health leads to more complex combined measures.

Conclusion

This is only the beginning of a journey to define the concept of health. But a preliminary observation must be that, even viewed objectively, it encompasses all these components – ill health includes disease, and illness, and sickness, and suffering, and physical or mental malfunctioning or trauma. But health is not simply the absence of these; it can be defined positively, and there may be other approaches to the concept. Moreover, as will finally be discussed in chapter 6, it is not a static concept but one which is still changing.

2
How is Health Constructed?

It has so far been assumed that health is a concept which is essentially 'factual', existing 'out there', even though it is multifaceted and may be looked at from various directions, and its causes and correlates may wait to be discovered. Discussion now turns to another view: that health, like all other human concepts, is an idea constructed by human agency.

Health as social construction

Medical philosophers have long pointed out that there is a sense in which even the concept of disease is an invention of humankind:

> All departments of nature below the level of mankind are exempt from both disease and from treatment ... The blight that strikes at corn or at potatoes is a human invention, for if man wished to cultivate parasites (rather than potatoes or corn) there would no 'blight', but simply the presence of man in a meaningful relation with them ... Outside the significances that man voluntarily attaches to certain conditions, there are no illnesses or diseases in nature ... Out of his anthropocentric self-interest, man has chosen to consider as 'illness' or 'diseases' those natural circumstances which precipitate the death (or the failure to function according to

certain values) of a limited number of biological species: man himself, his pets and other cherished livestock, and the plant-varieties he cultivates for gain or pleasure . . . Children and cattle may fall ill, have diseases, and seem as sick: but who has ever imagined that spiders or lizards can be sick or diseased? . . . The medical enterprise is from its inception value-loaded; it is not simply an applied biology, but a biology applied in accordance with the dictates of social interest. (Sedgwick 1973: 20)

This is an early representation of the position known as social constructivism, a major tradition of sociological thought which has had a profound influence in thinking about health. This proposes that reality is constructed through human action and does not exist independently of it. It is not suggested that phenomena are not 'real' and do not exist without our seeing them and ascribing meaning to them. But it is only human social activity which constitutes them as, for instance, health or disease. The social body influences the way in which the physical body is perceived and experienced.

How this construction happens is a special area of theory. In health, a major influence has been the sociological theory of symbolic interactionism developed in what is known as the Chicago School in the United States, largely from the work of Mead, between the two world wars and exemplified in the work of classic American authors in the 1960s and 1970s such as Blumer, Strauss and Goffman. Social reality is constructed by individuals interacting with one another on the basis of shared symbolic meanings: humans construct their behaviour, their relationships and their institutions in accordance with these interpretations and definitions. Thus health becomes what people, in interaction, define as health, and health institutions – such as that of medicine – are the creation of public discourses and definitions.

A weak view of constructivism is that it applies only, or particularly, to social issues: it would apply, for instance, to sickness and perhaps to illness, as previously defined, but not to disease. A 'strong' version sometimes implies that the world exists only in the head: there are no objective realities out there. Both of these are easily criticized. The more subtle position, and the one which has been dominant in medical sociology for three decades or so (though perhaps more strongly in Europe than in the United States), lies between the two. This approach holds that the world is at the same time objectively real *and* socially constructed. There is no suggestion that pathogens are not real, that disease does not exist, that pain is not a reality which can be described in neurological terms and experienced (even if differently from individual to individual) by the sufferer, or that attempts to demonstrate the regularities of epidemiology in numbers and rates are meaningless.

But, at the same time, health, disease and illness are, like every other human experience, social constructs; they are categories which have been named, defined and codified by human beings. The physical body which is their site may be 'given' – by God, by the laws of physical science, by heredity, or what you will – though even this is not absolute, since the body can also to some extent be 'constructed' socially. But disease or health, normality or abnormality, are *also* socially constructed categories which give meaning to classes of states and events.

What counts as disease or abnormality is not 'given' in the same sense as biological fact is given. It depends on cultural norms and culturally shared rules of interpretation. This is easier to accept in the case of illness, where it would seem obvious that there is immense room for individual interpretations and variations in behaviour: his cold is my influenza. But it must be emphasized that the approach goes beyond illness to include all processes, systems, categories of experience, in which humans are involved, and which are affected by their perceptions, intentions, choices and understandings.

The Polish philosopher and historian Ludwik Fleck was influential in proposing how 'received' knowledge is created and accepted. It is, he suggested, the outcome of a collective process of communication and interaction among 'thought collectives'. These are communities of people exchanging ideas, communities with a centre made up of specialists and a circumference of lay people. In the case of medicine, facts are established by the exchange and circulation of ideas and experience among scientists, doctors and patients. Knowledge is not simply that which is discovered by experts and then disseminated among the public, but something which is validated over time in overlapping networks.

In his book *Genesis and Development of a Scientific Fact* (1935), Fleck presented a case study of syphilis in these terms, and others have explored the ideas in more modern medicine. Arksey (1994), for instance, showed how, in the case of the diagnosis of repetitive strain injury, knowledge is shaped by social and cultural 'thought styles' of different clinical communities. Nicolson and McLaughlin (1988) offered a study of the disease multiple sclerosis, and Scott (1990) showed how the diagnosis of post-traumatic stress disorder became legitimated in the United States.

The 'construction' of disease is, of course, most easily demonstrated in such 'contested' diagnoses, where the biological basis is unclear or disputed. Nonetheless, a constructivist view would claim that it applies not only to these cases, but to disease as a general model.

Constructions of history

It can easily be demonstrated that what has been, and is, defined as health and illness has differed from era to era, and continues to differ from culture to culture. This is in part a matter of increasing scientific knowledge, of course, but not only that: disease has always existed, and always been universal, and biomedicine is a relatively recent development.

> Diseases are no more obvious a feature of the world than any other object of natural enquiry. Even if one supposes that natural kinds exist, separately from human classification, it seems unlikely that disease constitutes such a kind. Phenomena as disparate as hay fever and hysteria are assigned to this category because they inconvenience humans rather than because of any intrinsic similarities ... The rationality of diagnosis and therapy can only be understood in terms of the theory employed at the time, since it is always actors' categories that shape attitudes and actions. (Harley 1999: 417)

Symbolically, illness is one of the major ways in which individual and group misfortune is 'embodied'. Hence, it always calls for an explanation that goes beyond the search for causes and offers a 'truth' about both the order of the world and the body of the sick person. Illness has thus been said to be a metaphor. We cannot think of it, or its meaning, without at the same time thinking about the world and society (Herzlich and Pierret 1985).

Fabrega (1976a) offered an example of the anthropological or historical approach. He noted that the study of ancient populations shows that most of the major diseases now current have always been known to exist. Even if methods of controlling them have been achieved only recently, explanations and theories about them go back to prehistory. Rather than even 'primitive' beliefs being viewed as naive and superstitious, they should be seen as socially adaptive and part of a way of understanding the world. Primitive peoples, for instance, did not distinguish between medicine, magic and religion, and a framework of religion persisted throughout, and beyond, pre-literate times. Taxonomies included deities, powers, spirits – preternatural sources outside the individual. The ways in which they acted – witchcraft, forces of the environment – were also outside the individual, though the moral status of the individual very commonly had relevance.

The concept of diseases is continually changing: historians of medicine such as Engel (1963) have discussed how through the centuries the concepts and functions of medicine have oscillated between generalizations – the stuff of science – and concentration on the individual – the focus of medical therapy and what doctors actually do. The dichotomy goes back to the Platonic concept of universals or unchangeable realities, in opposition to the Aristotelian emphasis on the individual.

It is not only that science reflects and reproduces the dominant ideas of its time. The somewhat despairing residual definition of disease considered in chapter 1, that it is simply 'what doctors treat', does have some historical rationale. Society gives to medicine and healing as professions the task, in practice, of defining disease. How they perform it is affected not only by the advance of scientific knowledge but also by issues about their place in society. Jewson (1976) notably showed this by distinguishing three medical cosmologies, or schemes within which the medical profession operated, during the late eighteenth and the nineteenth century. In the first, which he called 'bedside medicine', doctors worked within an individually oriented cosmology where they were seeking for causes in terms of personal attributes. The second, object-related, cosmology began with the rise of the hospital, first in France in the early nineteenth century. Patients were no longer fee-paying and, largely, the more powerful sections of society: medicine had now ceased to be dependent on patronage, and control passed from the patient to the doctor. Interest turned to the pathology, rather than the patient: 'Interest in the unique qualities of the whole person evaporated' (Jewson 1976: 238). The third cosmology, laboratory medicine, arrived in the mid-nineteenth century, objectifying the patient altogether as a material thing. Thus changes in the conceptualization of health and disease are bound up with social relationships, and the development of medicine as a profession as well as a science.

What doctors treat as disease has clearly changed over time. For most schools of medicine in the ancient world symptoms were diseases of themselves. Ideas of disease as a syndrome, a constellation of related signs and symptoms, had existed in the Hippocratic school. The anatomists of the later eighteenth century converted the idea of a syndrome into anatomical features of the body, and throughout the nineteenth and twentieth century 'new' diseases were identified as new technology became available – a process which continues especially in the field of genetic medicine. Kendall was one of the commentators who described how each new advance in knowledge of physiology and each new wave of technology added new definitions of ill health to the accepted canon, and how some still survive incongruously. Many are recognized which are still only symptoms or syndromes. Others are based on bacteriology, histopathology, biochemistry and genetics. He offered a pleasant simile:

> In fact, the diseases we currently recognise are rather like the furniture in an old house, in which each generation has acquired a few nice pieces of its own but has never disposed of those inherited from its predecessors, so that amongst the inflatable plastic settees and glass coffee-tables are still scattered a few old Tudor stools, Jacobean dressers and Regency

> commodes, and a great deal of Victoriana. (Kendall 1975: 307)

Moreover, disease itself changes. Herzlich and Pierret (1987) pointed out that in each age one illness has dominated the reality of people's experiences – leprosy and plague in the Middle Ages, tuberculosis in the nineteenth century, and cancer and the chronic and degenerative diseases of industrialization in the twentieth century. These have become individualized again, in contrast to the epidemic infectious diseases of other times: they are the 'diseases of modern life'. And, of course, this process continues. The 'epidemiological transition', the change from predominantly infectious causes of death (still the pattern of poor countries) to the degenerative diseases which become the major forms of ill health in richer countries, continues and moves across the world. It also marks a change in the social distribution of many major conditions in richer countries. The best-known example is coronary heart disease, known as the disease of the rich in the mid-twentieth century, but now the disease of the poor. 'New' scourges such as HIV/AIDS are world-wide diseases with more of the character of the ancient 'epidemics', but (at least in the Western world) they are seen in a very individualized way. And of course (again, in the Western world) they are beginning to be seen, through therapeutic advances, as chronic diseases.

At the same time, there is historical continuity. Residues of older concepts of health and disease remain in medical practice and lay thought. For instance, the 'balance' that was the common idea in the Hippocratic corpus was primarily a theory of fluids or humours. Humoral theory, probably of more ancient origin but developed in the Greek and Arabic traditions, saw the body as a microcosm of the world, or Nature, whose elements were earth, air, fire and water. The four humours – blood, bile, black bile and phlegm – were linked to these, and to the four seasons, the four ages of man (childhood, youth, adulthood and old age) and the four primary qualities, hot, dry, cold and wet. Later scholars added such things as four colours, four tastes or the four evangelists (fig. 2.1). Each humour or combination of humours had its own diseases and its own remedies.

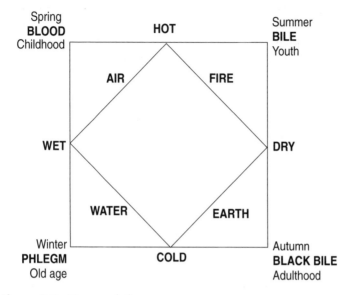

Figure 2.1 Humoral theory

This has proved to be one of the most persistent models throughout history. Echoes are left in the English language: bad-humoured, phlegmatic, full of bile, choleric, sanguine. In some non-Western or semi-Westernized medical systems, such as those of Latin America, the distinction between 'hot' and 'cold' disease is still central. In a Western society, Helman (1978) showed how ways of dealing with colds and fevers, in modern Britain, are influenced by the idea of harmony in the classical tradition. Disorders are still clearly classified by patients – and sometimes by their doctors – as hot or cold, wet or dry. The newer medical concept of germ theory is demonstrated in the patients' accounts of colds and fevers, but mixed with this very ancient idea of humours.

Another example is the idea of miasma. Very early in the history of medicine, ideas about the causes of disease, escaping the notion of malevolent gods and spirits, began to include the climate and natural forces. Bad air, or miasma, was the main cause of epidemic disease in the Hippocratic model. In medieval Western Europe, one cause of plague was held to be noxious vapours, miasmas, from stagnant pools, decaying corpses or the exhalations of the sick. As late as the eighteenth century, the conviction was still popular that sickness spread not from one person to another but from the environment to the individual. The bad environments of the slums of great towns, or of prisons and workhouses, generated bad air which triggered disease. This echoes still in contemporary thought, though we now know that in fact infectious and contagious disease is spread from person to person, and most ill health derives from causes within rather than outside the individual.

Constructions of culture

Illness is not only constructed by historical (and professional) processes and the advance of knowledge. It is also, clearly, shaped by cultural and moral values, experienced through interaction with other people and with institutions, and influenced by culture-specific beliefs.

> Nothing is more misleading than to consider the conditions of today's sick as the result of a linear evolution that always deals with the same physical realities, the same notions, the same values, and the same institutions. The transformation of the very nature of the principal diseases over time, the development of medicine with its false starts, its periods of triumph, and its explosion in the last century, the sudden linking of illness and work in the legal framework brought about by industrialization – all of these are examples of a restructuring of illness and the sick which show us that each society has its own way of letting the sick exist, defining them, and taking charge of them. (Herzlich and Pierret 1987: xii)

The definitions and categories provided by Western medicine form only one culturally based set. This is, of course, easy to demonstrate by reference to other times and other places. For instance, throughout human history up to recent times, and still, in poorer countries, the rich have been fat and the poor have been thin. In many societies obesity is attractive and a status symbol. In some pre-industrial societies the wives of important men were given especially fattening diets, for an ample body showed that they belonged to the section of society that experienced no shortages. It is only in Western societies, where the basic needs of the great majority of the population are met, and 'junk' diets which are fattening tend to be eaten less by the rich, that obesity becomes a disease and the aesthetics of body shape favour the slim.

Lest it should seem that all that is being said is that 'primitive' cultures lag behind, and have not yet reached the level of knowledge of modern Western societies, there are many contemporary examples from highly developed countries. Norms of what constitutes desirable states and behaviours are highly culturally influenced:

> There are, for example, countries where what Americans would call a defect in skin pigmentation is a sign of beauty and health. There are situations (where malaria is of high incidence) in which the sickle cell trait protects populations and sickle cell disease is sometimes said to be the necessary cost of that protection. There are combat situations wherein being color-blind is an advantage for spotting camouflage. There are contexts in which pregnancy is a disease state (*Brave New World*). The culture is (almost always?) at work. Masturbation, homosexuality, blacks' desire to escape slavery and flee to freedom, blacks' poor working habits on the plantations – all of these were each at one time classified as diseases in our culture. (Erde, 1979: 44)

Different societies, all subscribing to biomedicine, may have quite different medical systems: it has been said that 15 per cent of all biomedical diagnoses made in France are not shared with other Western cultures. An example is the common symptom syndromes of *triste* and *fatigué*, the present-day heirs of *accidie*, the sin of medieval times, which became 'melancholie' as the Church lost its power, and were subsumed in most Western cultures into psychiatric diagnoses. In non-Western societies many traditional, other, systems of belief exist and are part of formal medicine, side by side with Western biomedicine: examples include China, Africa, India and Japan. This may simply refer to the use of different therapies, especially drugs, but it may present very fundamental differences when (as in, for instance, China or Japan) issues such as the essential nature of life and death impinge on beginning- and end-of-life technology. For instance:

> Japanese attitudes to insensate things may offer some insights into the debate on brain death. The way in which machines in Japan are frequently 'animated' comes as a surprise to most outsiders . . . This attitude appears to be a direct legacy from the everyday lives of skilled workers of all kinds, whose activities have long been explicitly linked with Shinto ritual and with qualities of animism. Spirits reside not only in nature but also in tools and other instruments . . . Whereas in North America the thought of being attached in an unconscious state to a machine is humiliating and demeaning, quite different reactions are common in Japan. Rather than vizualize the machine as doing the work for the human, as taking over the empty shell, in Japan some people may conceptualize machine and human as working in partnership, creating an animated hybrid that can overcome all odds. (Lock 2002: 370)

On the other hand, many Western nations are increasingly adopting into their medical systems health beliefs and practices from other cultures. In the United States, for instance, this has included aspects of Chinese and Japanese herbal medicine, various sorts of meditation and healing techniques, acupuncture and many others.

At the same time, there are some concepts, quite outside biomedicine, which are remarkably pervasive throughout all eras and all societies. One of these is the moral framework imposed upon health and illness – more relevant, perhaps, to the way in which health is experienced (chapter 3) but still demonstrable as a cultural value in the medical systems of most societies. Another is a lingering faith in what was once described as magic or ritual, a causal system outside science. Treatment for diabetes, for instance, has been analysed in terms of the 'magical elements' in an orthodox medical system:

> 'The function of magic', Malinowski wrote, 'is to ritualize man's optimism'. Here we have doctors purporting to control diabetes, a metabolic disorder which they know involves a complex of biochemical parameters, through the manipulation of one such parameter over which they have incomplete

control. Further, they insist that maintaining 'good control' of this parameter is essential to the prevention or at least retardation of complications associated with the disorder. If they are not convinced they are doing the right thing, then they 'feel', 'believe', and 'hope' they are. They have faith in the efficacy of their ritual. (Posner 1977: 157)

Constructivism and feminism

That women's health has, throughout history and differently in different cultures, been 'constructed' within the relevant societies is clearly shown by feminist analyses. In a strictly biomedical model, differences between men and women can be referred to their biology. In a social model, the factually different circumstances of male and female lives may be held to account for differences in health. Differences in health-related attitudes or behaviour might be attributed to 'different' psychologies or cultural identities. Constructivist feminist approaches go further, however, in suggesting that women's health is in part a construct of the system of medicine, historically male-dominated:

> From the language used to describe female organs to the social and political theories of Western society women have been conceptualised as 'other'. Aristotle, for example, declared that women were constitutionally unfit for public life, whilst Rousseau stated 'It is of men that I am to speak'. Human nature as described by these and other thinkers (e.g. Aquinas, Machiavelli, Locke, Hegel) was intended to refer to male human nature ... Historically, this patriarchal ideology has permeated all social institutions, including science and medicine, where all states of women's reproductive lives are defined as potentially 'pathological' and thus in need of 'expert' (i.e. male) control. Throughout the scientific biological literature, the male body is seen as the 'norm' against which female bodies are measured and judged. (Williams and Bendelow 1998: 111)

The thesis is that this is an example of the definition of 'normal' functioning dictated by other than neutral scientific criteria. Men have controlled women's bodies and defined their healthiness. The myth of female frailty was used to justify women's exclusion from higher education until the twentieth century, and menstruation and, particularly, the menopause became medical 'problems'. Doctors supposed uterine and ovarian disorders to be behind almost every female illness, 'from headaches to sore throats' (Ehrenreich and English 1978: 123). Hysteria, the 'quintessentially female malady', has, for instance, been frequently discussed as the typical case of a constructed disease reinterpreted over the centuries and bound up with a view about women's nature and proper roles (Seale and Pattison 1994). In ancient Egypt and in Greece, and incorporated into the writings of Hippocrates, hysteria was a capricious female behaviour caused by the 'wandering' of the womb. Shifting views over the centuries reflected popular and medical ideas of the female character, its moral weakness and susceptibility to possession by evil spirits. In later centuries, with the rise of scientific medicine, hysteria became located in the brain and nervous system, or, following Freud, understood in entirely psychological terms, but still bound up with explanations involving the 'delicacy' and frailty of women. Some feminist historians have suggested that hysteria was in fact a method of protest for women who had no other outlets for self-expression, but others have seen it simply as a response to the frustrations of women's lives in the nineteenth century, or even a deliberate imposition of a label of pathology on rebellious behaviour. Throughout the twentieth century there was controversy over the diagnosis, now subsumed under a range of disorders not earlier recognized.

More generally, in recent times a feminist approach condemned, above all, the objectivization of women's bodies around their reproductive function and modern medicine's assumption of control over childbirth. Obstetrics and gynaecology constructed the normal experiences of pregnancy and childbirth in particular ways, especially as *medical* processes to be managed, and it was argued that some of the difficulties experienced by women in labour are in fact due to medical practices and the threatening hospital environment. This led to the movements to resist exposure to high-tech procedures in childbirth and the call for female-controlled alternatives to mainstream medical practice (Oakley 1976).

Illness as deviance

There are several special topics where many of these themes – cultural and societal contexts, the social construction of what ill health is, health as interaction, the age-old feeling that illness is a moral category and a deviation from some social norm – are specially visible. Mental illness, and chronic disease and disability, are fields where the theme of 'illness as deviance' and labelling theory have been prominent issues.

Labelling theory is a variant of symbolic interactionism, suggesting that 'deviance' is not the quality of the act the person commits but a consequence of the label that others apply to it. 'The deviant is one to whom the label has successfully been applied; deviant behaviour is behaviour that people so label' (Becker 1963). People defined as deviant – different from the norm, usually in a negative sense, as being less mentally fit than others, or having bodily impairments, or displaying disapproved-of behaviour – are labelled, stigmatized and segregated, and the behaviour which is a response to being treated in this way only feeds back to reinforce the label. Goffman, in the influential book *Stigma* (1967), analysed a three-stage stigmatization process: an initial or 'primary' deviation from some norm of behaviour, the negative reaction from others to this, and the stigmatized person's 'secondary' deviance in reply to the way in which they are treated by others. Freidson (1965) developed the concept of illness as deviance, adopting Becker's definition of deviance as rule-breaking behaviour, and taking up Goffman's and Lemert's distinction between primary and secondary deviation.

This is most obviously appealing in the sphere of mental health, where it has long been argued (notably by Scheff 1966) that whether behaviour is called 'mentally ill' depends on how others react to it: what psychiatrists call mental illness is largely simply a response to being labelled as insane and treated as 'deviant'. Less obviously, it can be argued that *all* illness can be seen as 'deviant', that is, differing from the norm of health in dysfunctional ways, and its existence depends on being recognized by others and acted out as illness.

Constructivism and mental illness

Constructivist approaches are easiest to accept in cases where great variation exists between cultures and societies and organic signs are lacking (as in some mental disorders, such as the example of schizophrenia in the USA and the UK). Mental illness was in fact one of the first areas where these ideas were applied, sometimes in extreme form. In the USA, Szasz was the best-known proponent of the view that the conditions psychiatrists treat did not exist in the same way as organic diseases. He claimed that in most cases it had never been demonstrated that there is a physiological abnormality in those called mentally ill, and their 'illness' simply consisted in behaving in ways which alarm or offend others, or in holding beliefs contrary to those usual in their society. In the UK, Eysenck suggested that the traditional field of psychiatry should be divided into a small medical part, including actual biological abnormalities or lesions, and a larger behavioural part. Another prominent name in this movement was Laing, who argued that schizophrenia, far from being a disease, was the only sane or rational way that some people have of coping with the stresses with which they are surrounded.

It is generally accepted that perhaps this goes too far. Many mental illnesses do exist as biological states, and most are more than simply a reaction to a label. Still, mental illness does remain as one of the clearest examples of how diseases can be constructed differently at different times and in different cultures.

Constructivism and disability

The ideas of constructivism and ill health as 'deviance' have been particularly important in the field of disability and chronic illness during the last half-century. Freidson was one of the early influential writers in the USA to point out that, like other stigmatized persons, people with disabilities tend to be evaluated as a category, rather than as individuals. Indeed, two stereotypes are usually involved, both predominantly negative: the label attached to the general category of 'disabled' and that which describes the particular impairment (crippled, blind). Since '. . . by definition, a person said to be handicapped is so defined because he deviates from what he himself or others believed to be normal and appropriate' (Freidson 1965: 72), then labelling, segregating and feed-back processes apply to the disabled as to other deviants. As sociologists went on to point out, there are problems about the concept of disabled people as a stigmatized minority group, and there are spokespeople for lobbies for disabled people who vigorously oppose the idea. However, these processes have clearly been illustrated for a range of visible and stigmatized conditions of the sort first, historically, defined as 'handicap' – disfigurements, epilepsy, sense deprivation. That a state of deviance may be created by the very agencies which are supposed to identify and help was demonstrated memorably by Scott (1966), who showed the relevant welfare agencies for the blind as engaged in '. . . a socialisation process, the purpose of which is to prepare a disabled person to play a type of deviant role' and construct blindness by 'making blind persons out of people who cannot see'.

The distinction between disease, illness and sickness discussed in chapter 1 is paralleled by the efforts of the WHO between their first 'International Classification' in 1980 of disabling conditions and their revision in 2000 to clarify the proper distinction between impairment (the physiological or psychological condition), disability (the functional consequences of this impairment) and handicap (the social consequences of disability). As one may be diseased without being ill, and ill without taking on the role of the sick, so one may have an impairment which is not disabling and a disability which is not, in any particular environment, or if it can be compensated for, a handicap. Disability is a field in which the nature of health as both biological *and* constructed is particularly obvious. Lobbies for disabled people have been energetic and successful in gaining acceptance of the viewpoint that it is society, not the condition, which disables; disability is

a relational phenomenon that emerges out of the interaction of a person with impairment and an 'environment' which includes everything from low income and inaccessible transport to a pitying glance from a passing stranger. (Williams and Busby 2000)

The critique of relativism

The ideas that have been illustrated have been much influenced by the contemporary movements called structuralism and post-structuralism. Structuralism (based largely on the work of the anthropologist Lévi-Strauss) analysed culture in terms of signs, codes and language. Post-structuralism, associated in health theory with the name of Foucault, particularly seeks to explain the social construction of bodies and emotions, and analyses in terms of power and knowledge, and the way the body becomes shaped, presented and socially evaluated.

Structuralism emphasizes the clear distinction which must be made between biological signs and their meaning as ill health (always remembering that it is not quite as clear-cut, since cultural meanings can easily translate, through physiological processes, into biological signs). This emphasizes the activity known as diagnosis, turning it into a process by which signs and symptoms are evaluated as having particular meanings, and their definition as ill health negotiated through interaction between people. Hence there has developed a large body of work in medical sociology on the process of medical diagnosis, observing the way in which a person comes to be defined as ill and entered into the status of a patient.

There have been various versions of the constructivist approach, the 'hardest' of which – denying the possibility of objective truth – has been subject to criticism. The suggestion that Western scientific medicine has no valid claim to special status, and that biological knowledge like any other is inevitably an ideologically based product of the society producing it, has been accused of not acknowledging the real advances of modern scientific medicine. The temptation to focus on contested diagnoses or mental illness, and underplay the importance of clear pathologies, may be accused of underestimating the burden of contagious disease in much of the world. To this extent the position can be said to be ethnocentric.

There is some argument that constructivism offers an 'oversocialized' view of individuals; that is, it does not allow for what sociology calls 'agency', or the exercise of (however restricted) free will by individuals, the way in which they act upon their surroundings rather than being acted upon. The position called critical realism, in particular, holds that social systems are open to process and change, and people have the critical capacity to act upon these structures.

Moreover, there is the argument that the 'hardest' version of relativism or constructivism cannot prove its own theses: if all systems of knowledge have equal status, then this, too, is only a partial and socially constructed view.

However, in 'softer' versions, to point to the cultural production of knowledge is not necessarily to undermine its practical value. The reality of suffering, or indeed the reality of healing, is not denied. Everywhere and in every successive era, healing requires a legitimated, credible and culturally appropriate system:

> For exorcist and possessed, or midwife and mother-to-be, or physician and patient, the relationship is created by semiotic, ritual and discursive acts, which are effective only in relation to specific cultural-symbolic and social-constructional circumstances. (Harley 1999: 433)

Certain kinds of practice may shape the development of particular kinds of knowledge: the use of a new model – from germ theory in the nineteenth century to the mapping of the human genome in our own time – may not simply reflect the social forces driving investigation at the time, but may lead to the selective perception of health phenomena. The 'medicalization' thesis is relevant here: this is the suggestion that the expansion of the universe of the things called illnesses is part of medical imperialism, a professional drive, both materially and intellectually motivated, to take over more and more of everyday life. It is also suggested by some commentators that contemporary medical knowledge is shaped by a class society (McKeown 1976): if social forces construct the nature of knowledge, then knowledge forms may evolve to serve ideological ends.

At the societal level, it seems indisputable that, throughout history and over different cultures, the concept of health has been shaped and constructed. New knowledge is one of the forces, and this continues as, contemporarily, new disease concepts arise because of new technologies. Further, it is suggested that, as new knowledge arises, new socio-technical relationships, including the commercial, drive the process on: this will be further considered in chapter 6.

3
How is Health Experienced?

Health is not just an observable, measurable property of a human body, and disease is not just the construction and diagnosis of medicine: they are subjective experiences. As Crawford (1984: 60) said,

> The body is not only a cultural object in illness or affliction. Bodily experience is also structured through the symbolic category of *health*. Health, like illness, is a concept grounded in the experiences and concerns of everyday life. While there is not the same urgency to explain health as there is to account for serious illness, thoughts about health easily evoke reflections about the quality of physical, emotional, and social existence. Like illness, it is a category of experience that reveals tacit assumptions about individual and social reality. Talking about health is a way people give expression to our culture's notions of well-being or quality of life. Health is a 'key word,' a generative concept, a value attached to or suggestive of other cardinal values. 'Health' provides a means for personal and social evaluation.

Lay concepts of health

Thus, the topic of lay concepts of health and illness has been the focus of very active research and discussion. Kleinman

(1980) distinguished three broad sectors of knowledge about health and illness:

- professional (orthodox, scientific, Western)
- alternative (folk, traditional, complementary)
- lay (popular, informal).

These overlap and their boundaries are, increasingly, flexible. Professional knowledge now includes much of the 'alternative'. Lay knowledge rests on both tradition and medical science. Indeed, it has been argued that, just as it is not practical to oppose illness and disease, so the label 'lay' concepts, though common as a shorthand, is not useful. Early definitions of lay attitudes to health, as those beliefs and practices explicitly derived from other cultural frames of knowledge, are not obviously applicable in modern Western societies, where lay accounts are usually filtered through internalized professional accounts. Lay beliefs can be better defined as commonsense understandings and personal experience, imbued with professional rationalizations.

The mid-twentieth-century interest in lay concepts was largely based on a wish to understand why people behaved as they did in choosing health-related actions or interacting with the profession of medicine. What 'folk' beliefs – especially among different ethnic or socio-economic groups – might intervene in efficient and 'compliant' collaboration with their doctors? Why was there resistance to medical procedures, or why were symptoms ignored? What 'wrong' beliefs required attention in health education?

If, in more recent decades, the approach to what is still called lay concepts is very much more complex, this is not to deny that (as discussed in chapter 1) residues of older or 'folk' concepts are still present in people's minds.

Treatment of a Cold or Chill is your own responsibility; it is your own problem, and is less likely to mobilise a caring community around you than a Fever. As in all Hot–Cold and humoural [*sic*] systems, treatment aims primarily to fight cold with warmth, and to move the patient from 'Cold' (or 'colder' than normal) back to 'normal', by adding heat in the form of hot drinks, hot-water bottles, rest in a warm bed, and so on;

and in giving him the means to generate his own heat, especially by ample warm food ('Feed a Cold, Starve a Fever'), as well as tonics and vitamins, which are also perceived as a type of nutriment. In addition, he must if necessary be shifted from the 'Wet' to the 'Dry' state – not by expelling or washing out the Fluids, but by drying them up. These Fluids are considered part of the body, and should be conserved, with the aid of nasal drops, decongestant tablets, inhalations, and drugs to solidify the loose stools. (Helman 1978: 117–18)

Moreover, their doctors may be complicit in trying to talk in folk terms: a patient who presents a list of symptoms is often given a diagnosis in the everyday idiom of the folk model: 'You've picked up a germ', 'It's just a tummy bug – there's one going around.'

Research on lay concepts now goes much further than this interest in folk ideas, however. It covers a number of essentially different questions. It may be, simply, how people (especially in different sections of society) define health. This is a difficult question to ask (or answer) in a direct form, and other issues may be used as indicators: what they see as the causes of ill health, how they think disease can be avoided, how they recognize other people as 'healthy', the accounts they give of their experiences of illness at particular times or over a life-time.

The questions may be asked by the qualitative method of interviewing people, in relatively unstructured or more structured ways, or by applying the methods of psychology such as tested 'instruments'. For large populations statistics can be applied to simple agree/disagree answers to statements about health, or some open-ended single question asking for a definition of health or combined answers to a range of questions about different aspects of health can be analysed. All of these are illustrated in the summary of research which follows. Each study may begin with different interests and hypotheses, and thus the analytic categories produced may be different: concepts of health cannot be 'reliably' measured in the same way as physiological or psychological attributes. Some common themes arise, however.

Lay definitions

A classic series of early studies was that of Claudine Herzlich in France in the 1960s, influenced by the work of Foucault and Muscovici's concept of 'social representations'. This approach to social psychology – examining the way in which individuals perceive the world as part of the more extensive systems of knowledge that society shares – saw subjectively perceived social representations both as the models which individuals use and as discourses in the public domain.

Herzlich (1973) identified three different metaphors to describe the way in which people talked about health and illness:

- *illness as destroyer*, involving loss, isolation and incapacity:

  If I were very seriously ill, if nothing more could be done, then it would be family life wouldn't exist any more . . . (p. 106)

- *illness as liberator*, a lessening of burdens:

  For me, illness is breaking off from social life, from life outside and social obligation, it's being set free.
  . . . It allows [people] to be what they were before and what they can't be because of social circumstances. (p. 114)

- *illness as occupation*, freedom from responsibility, except for the need to fight the disease:

  From the moment you know what's in front of you it seems to me the only thing to do is to gather your strength and fight. (p. 119)

Turning to more explicit representations of *health*, Herzlich found three, which could co-exist in one person's account:

- *health in a vacuum*, or the absence of illness, an impersonal condition, recognized only when one becomes ill

- *health as a reserve*, or physical strength and the capacity to resist illness, something inherited or the outcome of a good childhood, a characteristic of the individual which protects against becoming ill
- *health as equilibrium*, balance, harmony and well-being, contingent upon events in life, a state often under attack in modern society.

These three are sometimes discussed in terms of health as having, doing and being.

Other work, among different groups of people, has found similar categories. A study of middle-aged women in a Scottish city, and their daughters, both in poor socio-economic circumstances (Blaxter and Paterson 1982), found that health (especially for the older generation) was defined principally in terms of 'not being ill': health was either the absence of symptoms of illness, the refusal to admit their existence, the ability to define illnesses as normal ('at my time of life') or the determination not to 'lie down' to them. Health as a positive concept of well-being or positive fitness was absent in the older generation, and though their daughters were more conscious of fitness few had time or energy to devote much thought to it. A constant theme of these women's talk was the concept of illness as a state of spiritual or moral, rather than physical, malaise, associated with personality and a lack of moral fibre. If, in the face of this view, the experience of illness was inescapable – and, for the older generation in particular, it was – then the obvious residual category was one of health as simply chance.

Another study in Scotland (Williams 1990), of older people, found similar concepts to those of Herzlich, and similar emphasis on the moral and functional aspects of health. Health was defined as the absence of disease, and illness had to be coped with in five broad ways:

- as controlled by normal living, by keeping up normal activity
- as a continuous struggle
- as an alternative way of life
- as a loss to be endured
- as release from effort.

All the work considered so far has noted that the concepts of health derived must be considered in the light of the particular groups being studied. A different type of study has attempted to obtain definitions from large populations, with, usually, a particular interest in looking at the differences between groups. D'Houtard and Field (1986), for instance, reported on a very large survey in France which simply asked the question 'What is, according to you, the best definition of health?' The answers were analysed into forty-one different themes:

- for 'higher' and 'middle' classes, prominent themes were 'life without constraints', 'personal unfolding' and 'good physical equilibrium'
- for 'employees', they were 'watching oneself', 'being in a good mood', 'sleeping well', 'living as long as possible'
- for urban workers, themes were as for employees, but also particularly 'engaging in sports', 'having a normal appetite'
- for rural workers, they were 'being able to work', 'avoiding excess'.

In other words, those who did manual work found physical fitness and the ability to work to be key criteria, while those with non-manual occupations could see health as a more positive concept.

Another study in France, reported by Pierret (1993), used content analysis of both quantitative and qualitative methods with three sub-samples: residents of an 'old quarter' of Paris, residents of a 'new city', and farmers. The topic was introduced simply by 'I would like you to tell me about health, what it means to you.' Four 'registers' were found:

- health-illness, talk organized around health as not being ill
- health-tool, an impersonal view of health as a capital that everyone has, the principal form of wealth, to be used as a tool
- health-product, health as a personal value, with controllable and uncontrollable factors held in balance
- health-institution, health seen from a collective and political viewpoint, to be managed by society.

Which of these was favoured appeared to be related to the individual's social and occupational position. For instance, public-sector wage-earners tended to express health as collective and governmental; manual workers saw it in terms of not-illness or as a tool; farmers' illness and risk beliefs fell into a homogeneous world-view based on a cycle of life over which they had some control. Pierret observed that, 'In France, persons' relations to the State, in particular whether they work in the private or public sector, seem to be as important as social class origins' (1993: 22).

A nation-wide UK study, *Health and Lifestyles* (Blaxter 1990), posed a similar open-ended question: 'What is it like when you are healthy?', also asking people to describe 'a healthy person' whom they knew. Replies were analysed to form five main categories:

1 *Health as not-ill* Here health is defined by the absence of symptoms or lack of need for medical attention, for example:

Health is when you don't hurt anywhere and you're not aware of any part of your body. (woman of forty-nine)

A healthy person is someone who hasn't seen a doctor for fifty years. (woman of seventy, speaking of her husband)

Health was clearly distinguished from disease. One might be diseased, and ill, and therefore unhealthy, but equally one could be healthy despite disease: 'I am very healthy apart from my arthritis.' This definition of health was found to be a little more frequently used by the better educated and those with higher incomes, and was markedly associated with the speaker's own state of health. Those who themselves were in poor health were much less likely than those in good health to use the not-ill definition.

2 *Health as physical fitness, vitality* Among younger people, health as physical fitness was very prominent. Young men, in particular, stressed strength, athletic prowess and the ability to play sports; 'fit' was by far the most common word used in these descriptions of health by men under forty. Women and older men used the word 'energy': sometimes physical energy was meant, and sometimes a psychosocial

vitality which had little to do with physique, but often the two were combined. This, and the idea of 'healthy though diseased', has some affinity with Herzlich's 'health as reserve'. This concept was often expressed in ideas of heredity, or resistance, or recovering quickly from illness, for example:

> Both his parents are alive at ninety so he comes of healthy stock. (woman of fifty-one)
>
> Health is when I feel I can do anything . . . nothing can stop you in your tracks. (man of twenty-eight)
>
> Health is having loads of whump. You feel good, you look good, nothing really bothers you, life is wonderful, you seem to feel like doing more. (woman of twenty-eight)

3   *Health as social relationships* Social relationships were also frequently associated with this definition of health, though almost always by women rather than men. For younger women, health was defined in terms of good relationships with family and children; for the elderly, this was redefined as retaining an active place in the social world and caring for others, for example:

> You feel as though everyone is your friend. I enjoy life more, and can work, and help other people. (woman of seventy-four)

4   *Health as function* Both health as energy and health as social relationships overlap with the idea of health as function – health defined as being able to do things, with less emphasis on a description of feelings. Health as function was more likely to be expressed by older men and women; the ability to cope with the tasks of life might, of course, be taken for granted among younger people. For men particularly, health was bound up with pride in being able to do hard work. For the elderly, health could mean being mobile, or self-sufficient, able to care for themselves or to continue to work, despite the inevitable ills of old age:

> Health is being able to walk around better, and doing more work in the house when my knees let me. (woman of seventy-nine)

5   *Health as psychosocial well-being* This category was reserved for expressions of health as a purely mental state, instead of, or as well as, a physical condition. It was, in fact, the most common definition of health among all age groups except young men, and a definition expressed by over half of middle-aged women. It tended to be used rather more by those with higher education or non-manual jobs. It was a very holistic concept: 'happy', 'confidence', 'enjoying life' were words used to describe it, and 'health is a state of mind' or 'happy to be alive' were common statements. Examples of this definition of health include:

> . . . physically, mentally and spiritually at one. (woman aged forty-five, living in a religious community)
>
> Emotionally you are stable, energetic, happier, more contented and things don't bother you so. (woman aged twenty, secretary)
>
> I've reached the stage now where I say isn't it lovely and good to be alive, seeing all the lovely leaves on the trees, it's wonderful to be alive and to be able to stand and stare. (farmer's widow, aged seventy-four)

The way in which health was defined over the life-course differed, in not unexpected ways. There were also clear gender differences. At all ages, women gave generally more expansive answers than men and appeared to find the questions more interesting. These definitions were not exclusive, and many people combined several of the categories.

Self-rated health

Another large body of work which is relevant is that which seeks to understand why people define their own health as they do, when, in surveys, they are asked to categorize it as (usually) 'excellent, good, fair or poor, compared with someone of your own age?' This 'self-rated health' question is an extremely common one, in attempts to 'measure' and compare the health of groups or populations, and, though it may seem too vague and subjective to be of great use, in fact it has been shown to match remarkably well, at the population level, with other more objective measures, and even to predict population mortality rates. However, at the individual level there are of course anomalies, and for many decades there has been study, especially in Scandinavian countries, Israel and the United States, of what these are, and whether they are socially patterned in any way that might be predictively useful. That some people may insist they are in excellent health, when by all objective standards their health would be described as poor, and others insist on poor health for which there appears to be no evidence, may say something about the way in which the concept is being defined.

In the *Health and Lifestyle Survey* self-definitions of health as good or poor were strongly associated with the concepts of health described earlier. The concepts of not-ill and of health as fitness were more likely to be used by those who thought that their own health was good, especially among men: there was, of course, an association with youth (and probably better health) and the choice of 'fitness', but at all ages those who chose this concept were more likely to be the self-defined healthy. Women who offered a definition of health in terms of psychosocial well-being were also more likely to take a positive view of their own health. Differences between social groups showed strongly in self-assessments, with the poorest and most disadvantaged most likely to say that their health was poor, especially in older years. Single parents, those living in areas of high urbanization, and the unemployed were also more likely to call their health poor, to an extent greater than compatible with the objective health measures. States such as depression, and personality traits such as neuroticism, were also associated with what seemed to be unduly pessimistic self-assessments.

It is common to note that by far the majority of people, asked this question, define their own health as excellent or good, though almost everyone can tick symptom lists and most, in discussion, will talk about their ailments rather than their health. This is usually explained as an indication of health as a social norm, a desirable characteristic to lay claim to if one is asked to describe oneself in a single word. More unexpected is the common finding that many people will describe their health as good even in the face of severe impair-

ment or serious chronic disease. This is particularly true of
the elderly. It seems that these people are saying 'my health
is excellent considering my years', or 'my health is excellent
despite my disability.' Health is displayed as a relative concept, highly dependent on expectations.

This is demonstrated in many of the in-depth studies where
people talk about their health histories. A self-definition of
good health despite evidence to the contrary can represent a
positive determination to distinguish impairment from ill
health – 'I may be in a wheelchair but I can still call myself
healthy.' It may also represent a normalization of health
hazards in the past:

> My health was all right. I had diphtheria and pneumonia and
> all that sort of thing. There used to be a lot of that then. But
> my health was good. (woman talking of her childhood in the
> 1930s in a family of ten children; Blaxter 2002)

Concepts of the causes of health and illness

A sixth, albeit minority, definition of health found in the
population survey could only be called 'health as a healthy
life'. It was expressed in terms of health being 'eating a
healthy diet, and not smoking and drinking', and was
excluded from the previous discussion because it was judged
not to be an answer to the question. Faced with this difficult
task of definition, some people retreated to answering an
easier question: What causes good health? Because it *is* an
easier question on which to present lay views, it is one which
has perhaps been asked more frequently than 'What is
health?', and one on which there is a long history of research
and discussion. Of course, what people believe are the causes
of disease and the ways of ensuring health may also say something about their definition of the concept itself.

Remembering the practical service-use focus of the earliest
studies (and with the mid-twentieth development of the psychosocial model of health also relevant), the focus of much
of the early work, especially in psychology, was on whether
health and its causes were seen as *internal* or *external* to the

individual. A psychological construct known as the *health locus of control*, specifically applying social learning theory to the way people explain health and illness, divided people into 'internals', who saw health and illness as the outcomes of their own attitudes and behaviour, and therefore in their own hands, and 'externals', who saw them as the consequences of outside influences or simply chance. The importance of the distinction is, of course, that the two groups might behave very differently in relation to their health. Though this simple division was soon seen as crude, and various more elaborated concepts were developed in psychology, nevertheless the internal/external, or psychosocial and behavioural/material, distinction has been a very constant theme.

In a number of studies in the 1980s Pill and Stott (1982, 1987) used these concepts to examine the health beliefs of Welsh 'lower-working-class' mothers. A 'salience of lifestyle' index was used to distinguish between *lifestylists* and *fatalists*. Those with a low 'salience of lifestyle' were people who denied any blame or personal responsibility for illness; with a medium level they ascribed illness to stupid or careless behaviour; and with a high level they believed that good health is a product of willingness to adopt healthy habits and comply with preventive measures. The 'lifestylists' spontaneously mentioned taking health-promoting actions and had better health knowledge; the 'fatalists' saw health as a matter of being able to 'keep going' and fulfil their obligations, and relied upon their doctors.

The accounts of the elder generation of Scottish women discussed earlier were analysed to look more widely at their concepts of 'cause' (Blaxter 1983). A content analysis of their descriptions of their lives and their health selected out each disease or illness mentioned, and what cause was being ascribed to it, in order not to consider how 'accurate' their knowledge was, but trace out the structure of their causal thinking. All the illnesses or diseases they mentioned could be placed in the following categories, in order of 'popularity':

1   *Infections and agents in the environment* The prominence of infections, given that the topic of conversation was

often children, and remembering the prevalence of infectious disease at the time of these women's childhoods in the 1920s or 1930s, was easily understood, but the external environment could also include climate, pollutants or working conditions.

2 *Heredity or familial tendencies* These (not always distinguished) were given much more weight than medical science might allow: 'We're all made of an impression on our ancestors, aren't we?'

3 *Disease secondary to other diseases or to trauma or surgery* This prominent category of cause related to what appeared to be seen as assaults upon the body, chains of illnesses, anything which might leave weaknesses or gaps in defences: 'Once you're opened up the cold sets in.' Childbearing (these women had large families, often unwillingly) left them with a stock of stories to prove that 'a woman's never the same when she's had children.' Drugs and, especially, the contraceptive pill were also blamed for illness.

4 *Stress and psychological explanations* These women were very conscious of the mind/body link, and almost any disease could be attributed, at least in part, to stress: 'It's because I am a worrier', 'It's a nervous trouble.'

5 *The constraints of poverty and neglect* The undoubted material causes of ill health in these women's lives – poor housing, poverty, physically harmful work – came rather low down in their list of causes for disease. Rather, they spoke of neglecting their health, but not in an irresponsible way. Life circumstances made care of one's health and treatment for one's illnesses impossible: 'In those days, you didn't think about it – you had to be there, you had kids to feed, a house to keep, and that was it.'

6 *Inherent individual susceptibility* Among the less popular categories of cause, inherent susceptibility – not hereditary or familial – was blamed. The sufferer was in a sense responsible for these illnesses, but given one's personal make-up there was nothing that could be done to avoid them: 'I'm just the type.' There was a common concept of 'readiness' to take disease.

7 *Voluntary behaviours* The instances of women being willing, clearly, to blame their own behaviour were rela-

tively few, though the consequences of overweight and of smoking were acknowledged.

8 *Natural degeneration and ageing* A conspicuous feature of the women's general norms of health was an acceptance of poor health as a natural feature of the ageing process, and an accelerated time-scale for 'getting on now': 'See, I'm getting on in years, so I'm not really bothered now. See, I'm 47 . . . If they canna do nothing about it, they canna do nothing about it.' However, few specific diseases or ailments were attributed to the ageing process. Things which 'just happened' were also conceptually avoided: randomness and inevitability alike were threatening.

Like the Welsh women mentioned earlier, these were a special group, and in both cases it was pointed out that the circumstances of their lives were relevant to their concepts of cause. Pill and Stott argued that what, from one point of view, may be seen as fatalism, may, from another, be interpreted as a realistic appraisal of the causes of their ill health.

Attempts to look at the causal concepts not of special groups (and especially more disadvantaged groups) but among the population more generally have been made in different ways. Stainton Rogers (1991), for instance, derived attitudes to causes from interviews by the method know as Q-sort: that is, asking people to sort a number of statements supplied to them which, as far as possible, reflect the broad range of generally available ideas and arguments about a concept. Distinct themes or 'alternative accounts' were identified, representing the different ways in which people thought about the causes of health. For instance, three of these were the 'body as machine' account, regarding illness, within the medical model, as naturally occurring and 'real'; the 'willpower' account, which saw the individual as pre-eminently in control, and stressed moral responsibility; and the 'robust individualism' account, which was concerned with the individual's right to choose how to live their lives. All are explained within the interplay between the individual and society, but some models assume that individuals have a choice about their living conditions and that health status is a product of individual circumstances and decision-making, while others see lives as largely constrained and defined by their social position. Stainton Rogers also pointed out that, whether health causes are being seen as external or internal, different types of explanation may be invoked for good health and for bad health.

At the level of a population, the *Health and Lifestyle Survey* in the UK (Blaxter 1990) was used to attempt to derive models of cause. People were asked series of questions about the causes of specific diseases, about what they thought made their own lives healthy or unhealthy, and why it was thought that 'people' – i.e., society at large – were healthier or unhealthier 'nowadays'. The answers to a great many questions were amalgamated to form categories of causal beliefs. In particular, the analysis asked whether different groups of the population were more or less likely to think of health as outside the individual's control or as their own responsibility, whether they thought about the causes of health differently in different contexts, and whether their own health status and experience, as documented in other parts of the survey, affected the way in which they thought about causes.

In the context of a 'survey' about health – and the issue of different ways of 'accounting' for health will be discussed later – 'behaviour', in the form of diet, smoking, exercise, drugs, alcohol consumption, was presented as the major cause of both good and bad health, by all ages and social groups: the lessons of health education about self-responsibility appeared to be well learned. 'Medical' causes – scientific advance, new drugs, medical care, better education – were also prominent as causes of good health, but more among the young and the better educated. 'External' causes – work, public health on the one hand or pollutants and poor environments on the other – were less frequently favoured. Stress, pace of life and other psychosocial factors were frequently mentioned for negative aspects of health: almost every disease offered could be caused by 'stress'. There was, of course, a long list of other, less common, categories, but one which is perhaps notable was that poverty and prosperity, general standard of living, was mentioned much more as one of the categories for *good* health, but less as a source of illness (particularly among the elderly and the poorer groups who might be expected to be the more vulnerable).

It was also notable that the concepts of health and illness seemed generally to be viewed differently depending whether the focus was on the experience of health, or illness and disease. Moreover, people had different concepts depending on the contextual frame. Where the questions were about specific, named diseases, behavioural answers were overwhelmingly predominant: poor diet or lack of exercise, together with stress, could be the cause of almost any chronic disease. In the context of their own health and their own lives, rather fewer gave this type of answer, as might be expected: the causes of their own ill health were individual and complex, and not necessarily wholly their own fault. That structural or economic factors such as poverty or the external environment were crucial was mentioned relatively frequently for society at large, very infrequently in the context of one's own health or illness, and barely at all as the causes of specific diseases.

The search for meaning

Some general conclusions may be drawn from the studies which have been described. Firstly, health and illness are not simply opposites. Good health has qualities that go beyond the simple absence of disease or illness and is logically independent of them. Concepts of health – whether described as equilibrium, as reserve or as psychological happiness – connect with other areas of life. Health is, at the least, keeping going, performing one's everyday activities, irrespective of disease, and at the best it is a wholly psychosocial or spiritual state of well-being.

Secondly, the importance of cause in concepts of health and illness is obvious. Asking people to discuss 'health' very frequently soon merges into their accounts of the cause of illness. For those who are experiencing illness, to understand the causes is their most basic concern. As Herzlich and Pierret (1987: 100) noted, medicine has never, perhaps, 'provided a totally satisfactory answer to the questions Why me? Why now?' These questions

> demand an interpretation that goes beyond the individual
> body and the diagnosis. The answer that is given transcends

the search for causes and becomes a search for meaning. We still want to fit illness into the order of the world and of society.

People's beliefs about cause affect their interpretation of their symptoms and what they are likely to do about them. Koos (1954), in a very early study in the USA, documented the reasons for the health actions of the people of 'Regionville'. Just as one of these respondents said: 'If I knew how I did it – say, from lifting a bucket of coal – I might not go [to the doctor] as quick as if I didn't know where it came from', so the Scottish women of Blaxter (1983) would say things such as 'If I got another pain I would just take it was the menopause again.' These and all the other accounts of health histories are full of people worrying over symptoms, perhaps consulting again or in a different way, because, although they had been given a diagnosis, they had not been given a *cause*, or at least one which they found acceptable.

A third general point which seems to arise concerns the complexity of people's thinking. Talk about health and illness cannot be expected to be consistent and lack any contradictions, because different views are held in different contexts. Descriptions of interview research (or, indeed, other data such as autobiographies) show that replies to simple survey questions about what they 'believe' should really take the form of 'it all depends', 'yes and no', 'sometimes this and sometimes that'. People think of health differently when the context is their own health (about which they have, of course, detailed knowledge) or that of other people, and whether they are directed to think about health as some general concept or as specific forms of disease.

A fourth general point is that people's models of health are commonly holistic, involving body and mind. The principle of 'mind over matter' appears again and again. To be healthy is to be happy, and the causes of many – perhaps most – illnesses lie in the psychosocial realm. Pollock, studying families in an English city, noted that 'mental attitude was thought to influence both susceptibility to illness and its outcome, while a sick body could also produce illness in the mind' (1993: 51). A very high proportion of respondents stressed the importance of attitude of mind:

You can make yourself healthy or you can make yourself unhealthy. You can work for or against health. It's all in the mind. (1993: 53)

This was echoed by many statements from the respondents of Stainton Rogers (1991: 193):

I am firmly convinced that I have considerable power to influence my own health . . . I believe that disease can often be held off – it is never purely physical . . . One should have sufficient control over oneself to prevent one from getting ill.

Health as moral discourse and metaphor

Several of these general findings relate to the theme of health as moral discourse. The association of illness with weakness, sin and punishment has, apparently, some permanence, and is associated with ideas of faith, submission, and the redemptive power of suffering.

Herzlich was one of the first to point out that to think of oneself as healthy is to think of oneself as in a particular relationship to society. Proof of good health is proof that one is a worthy and responsible person, and, particularly for working-class people, fitness of the body defines both healthiness and commitment to work. Cornwell (1984), interviewing London families, identified the duty to keep working and not 'give in' or seek help until it was impossible to continue as a key concept of working-class culture. However, in all social groups there are contemporary pressures to identify health with youth, strength and independence – positive cultural values which mean that one is unwilling to admit to being intrinsically 'unhealthy'.

The metaphor of fighting illness, not 'lying down' to it, overcoming adversity, is pervasive in accounts of illness in Western society. Self-responsibility is specially strong among those suffering from chronic conditions. Pollock (1993), for instance, showed how responsibility to maintain health is regarded as a duty not only to oneself but also to families, the wider community and perhaps a higher authority. These attitudes derive from a Judeo-Christian culture underpinned by both altruism and autonomy. Women, especially, have a moral duty to manage illness because they care for others, but for everyone, moral character is assessed through the response to ill health and adversity. Williams (1993) similarly demonstrated that it is not so much health itself which is seen as virtuous, as the self-discipline which not only responds to it but also produces it. The presence of health reflects correct behaviour, self-discipline, willpower and virtue, and its absence is a sign of weakness. 'Fighting' illness is a way of talking about it which is strongly culturally approved.

It is debatable how far these moral attitudes to health can be seen as a universal mode of human thinking, with many parallels in the anthropological literature, and how far they mirror what Sontag (1979) has called the 'particularly modern predilection for psychological explanations of disease, as of everything else'. Sontag perceived this as something imposed by society on sufferers, undermining the reality of disease, but it may be that it is one more way of locating the cause of illness outside the body.

Health may be seen very fundamentally by individuals as part of identity, but illness is perceived as something both inside and outside the body. To the extent that it enters and takes over, it becomes part of the self. At the same time, it is an invasion. It is a common theme in medical sociology that illness is thought about, and talked about, in objectified or metaphorical terms. Disease is 'it', separated from the body, and by extension parts of the body also become 'it', not 'me': 'it went to the stomach.' Williams (1996) has commented on the way in which, in health, we take the body for granted. In illness, this unity is disrupted and the body becomes separate from the self.

Metaphors may range from the moral world, with disease talked of as 'evil', to a mechanical image, with the heart, for instance, spoken of as an engine. Herzlich and Pierret (1987) in France, and Sontag (1979) in America, have written of the way in which, historically, diseases become metaphors themselves: TB of passion, cancer of repression, first cancer and then AIDS in military or even Star Wars language of the body as a fortress and the illness as an invading enemy.

Responsibility for health

Several of these ways of looking at how health is experienced feed into one of the most debated issues about subjective health: on the one hand the question of self-responsibility, health as the consequence of one's own character or behaviour, and on the other illness as imposed, involuntarily, by the material world. There is an obvious tension between the universal wish to externalize and objectify disease and the intensely moral and psychosocial model of health so often expressed. Whether people will take responsibility for their health, and how they may vary by social groups, is an issue in which those responsible for health policy, health services and health care are clearly interested.

One particular theme of all the work on lay beliefs is the demonstration that how people think about health and illness varies with their place in society. The concepts of locus of control, and lifestylists and fatalists, discussed earlier, are relevant. In general, middle-class people have been said to view illness in terms of mental attributes and attitudes, and be more likely to see themselves as having more 'internal' control; the working class to view health more in physical and functional terms and to lack a sense of control. Blair (1993), for instance, showed how the middle class are more likely to use emotional and psychological experiences in talk about health, and focus more on the role of self, while the working class use more physically located experiences and place less emphasis on personal control.

This may, as Blair points out, have more to do with language and available forms of expression than with fundamental ways of thinking. But it has long been suggested that health has a more positive value for the middle class or more educated (who are the greater consumers of health-oriented products) than for the working class (who are said to be focused more on 'instant gratification' or, more practically, have less time, money or energy to devote to health-enhancement). This has been invoked as a cultural explanation for the lesser use of preventive services by poorer groups of the population.

However, throughout the literature, the mind-over-matter theme is expressed not only by the educated and articulate but also by many in poor circumstances, who might be expected to prefer to blame more the disadvantages which were not under their control. This, and the reluctance to subscribe to the 'inequality in health' thesis, has been tentatively explained in terms of their wish to present their moral identity. Opprobrium is attached, not to *having* illness, which may be unavoidable and not their own responsibility, but to 'lying down' to it. The Scottish women whose concepts of health were presented earlier were

> perfectly capable of holding in equilibrium ideas which might seem opposed: the ultimate cause, in the story of the deprived past, of their current illhealth, but at the same time their own responsibility for 'who they were'; the inevitability of illhealth, given their biographies, but at the same time guilt if they were forced to give in to illness. (Blaxter 1993: 141)

Their life histories were their evidence that, though they had no great material prosperity to offer, nevertheless they could justify themselves. People in all social groups can similarly be at once 'victims' – that is, present themselves as suffering particular stresses – and at the same time be proud of the inner strength that enables them to cope. Stories of illness in terms of moral virtue, as Williams (1993) shows, reveal the ill person's view of society and their place in it.

Martin (2000) has suggested that for everyone, not only the poor, there are contemporary paradoxes in accepting responsibility for health. Ordinary people are now being taught to see their bodies not as a set of mechanical parts but as complex non-linear systems – fluid, changing, unstable, in delicate relationship with their environment. This may leave them feeling 'responsible for everything and powerless at the same time, a kind of empowered powerlessness':

> Imagine a person who has learned to feel at least partially responsible for her own health, who feels that personal habits like eating and exercise are things that directly affect her health and are entirely within her control. Now imagine such

a person gradually coming to believe that wider and wider circles of her existence – her family relationships, community activities, work situation – are also directly related to personal health. Once the process of linking a complex system to other complex systems begins, there is no reason, logically, to stop. (Martin 2000: 131)

Health histories and health capital

Lay accounts of health history are a fruitful source of models of lay thinking about the meaning of health and illness. They usually show, for instance, a clear appreciation of the fact that causes are not simple, and that a clear dichotomy between 'behaviour' and 'material conditions' is not sustainable. There is usually a notable strain towards linking chains of cause together in a logical fashion, whether or not the links are sustainable biomedically. For the Scottish women, it was suggested that, although they appreciated that disease might sometimes strike randomly, they resisted the idea that one part of their body might 'go wrong' at one time, and another at another time, without there being any connection. One thing must lead to another: there must be a logical biography. These chains of cause stretched back through generations:

> This fondness for familial explanations, for connecting up the events of their lives, could be understood as a liking for continuity, a desire to give meaning to their lives. Their family histories, together with their own experiences, constituted their identity. Their present health status, including all the emerging problems of middle age, had to be accommodated into that identity. (Blaxter 1993: 138)

In talk about their health, people often use (though not, of course, explicitly) the simple metaphor of *health capital* (Blaxter 2000). As economic capital is represented by the accumulation and loss of monetary value, so health capital consists of currency in terms of fitness, strength, immune status, inherited characteristics, physical damage and vulnerability. A genetic stock is laid down at conception, and *in utero*, at birth and in early childhood it is elaborated and a basis for life-long health provided. Throughout life capital is lost, by health-damaging events and circumstances, by behaviour such as smoking, by the dangers and stresses of childbearing and of work, and by simple accident and the degradations of time. It can also be added to, by 'healthy' behaviour, favourable life circumstances, and even good luck.

Some perception of this concept – particularly relevant to the social inequalities in health discussed in chapter 5 – is clear in people's accounts. Heredity and familial patterns are a pervasive theme. For many poor city-dwellers a 'healthy' rural childhood is the foundation of their survival, even where the actual circumstances appeared to be unhealthily characterized by deprivation and family histories torn apart by the old infectious diseases. For them, a rural childhood in a golden past represented health capital, though depleted since by specific events and stresses. Working histories and, for women, childbearing are salient for long-term health. Most reported health histories are bound up, subjectively, with a long and intricately worked-out series of previous events and circumstances.

Illness as narrative: health and illness accounts

Discussion of concepts of health has inevitably turned to narratives of illness. Health is not, in fact, easy to talk about. In the national survey of health and illness (Blaxter 1990) over 10 per cent of the population, asked baldly for a definition of health, could give no reply. These were more likely to be the young, and men, who might respond, 'I can't answer that', or 'I just don't think about it.' There is some danger in assuming that this is a negative or uninterested attitude to health, since it may be no more than a lack of enthusiasm for the interview situation. Illness and its causes are easier to talk about than an abstract notion of health, and one's own illness easiest of all. Illness narratives are common in research, in literature and in journalism, and of recent decades the analysis of their form and structure has been a topic of interest. Accounts of illness experience concern more than simply a physical or mental condition and its causes and consequences, but articulate the individual's situation in the world.

Bury (2001) points out that this interest in lay narratives arose in part because of the growing impact in modern times of degenerative and chronic illness, where 'the contingencies of everyday life reassert themselves, and the subjective patient view becomes audible once more' (p. 267). The loosening of the biomedical grip provides the space for lay narratives to flourish. Also, the promotion of holistic medicine and the value of 'listening to the patient' mean that patient narratives can demand attention. The expansion of public information about illness 'provides lay people with a much greater opportunity to fashion personal narratives that connect the private sphere with the public forms of knowledge' (p. 268).

Bury identified three types of narrative form: *contingent narratives*, which address the immediate causes of an illness episode and its effects on everyday life; *moral narratives*, which provide accounts of changes in social identity and help to establish the moral status of the individual; and *core narratives*, which reveal connections between the person's experience and deeper cultural meanings attached to health and illness.

Frank (1995), in his book *The Wounded Storyteller*, has similarly argued that, as acute illness gives way to chronic, individuals need to make sense of their experience, learn from it, 'tell their stories'. Stories do not just describe the experience: they are repair work, creating a new self. Published illness narratives were analysed to understand the cumulative changes in the self found there, and three types of narrative were distinguished:

- restitution, or effort towards cure and the restoration of the healthy self
- quest, or self-transformation into a new self
- chaos, describing a life that will never get better.

Serious illness is a loss of the 'destination and map' that had previously guided the ill person's life, and ill people have to learn to think differently: 'they learn by hearing themselves tell their stories' and by the reactions of others to them. Particularly in postmodern times, people feel 'a need for a voice they can recognise as their own.' Stories are of course premodern, an ancient way of transmitting culture and making sense of the world, but the traditional narratives of experiencing misfortune and illness become lost within modern biomedicine:

> The postmodern experience of illness begins when ill people recognise that more is involved in their experiences than the medical story can tell. The loss of a life's map and destination are not medical symptoms, at least until some psychiatric threshold is reached. (Frank 1995: 17)

As Hyden (1997) noted, since narrative is the way in which we come to know and make sense of the social world, it is important to pay attention not only to *what* people say – the accuracy or not of the account of the temporal world – but also to *how* they say it, the way in which they construct this world.

The interpretation of illness narratives is not without problems, however. Accounts of illness, in the forms available for analysis, are interactions between the individual and an audience. Narratives can be first-person or third-person stories. They also have different functions: to construct the new world of illness or the new identity, to reconstruct a previous life history or, strategically, to explain or make use of the illness. They can also be used to transform individual experience into collective experience. Illness narratives, like others, have conventional forms: the cause and effect of change, or the 'questing' plot described by Frank (1995), is a common one, in which the narrator emerges through the illness as a new person. Good (1994) pointed out, however, that illness stories have the particular quality of being ambiguous, in that they lack that prerequisite of a story, an end. In the illness narrative there are always possibilities of a different ending: the narrative of health is continually renegotiated.

It is generally argued (Radley and Billig 1996) that we should talk of 'accounts', rather than the concepts or beliefs that narratives display. Cornwell's (1984) early distinction between 'public' and 'private' accounts has been influential. In her interviews, public accounts were those which reproduced what was interpreted as 'real' knowledge as legitimated by expert opinion; these were the kinds of account which would generally be offered in the setting of a formal interview. Private accounts, on the other hand, appeared to arise out of personal experiences, and were usually offered in a less formal setting. This was not simply the difference between 'medical' and 'lay' models, since each could be included in both accounts. Public accounts were 'social representations', shaped largely by medicine; private accounts were personal narratives, which might include social representations to a greater or lesser degree.

Accounts of illness are accounting for a self, but offer a dilemma for the speaker: the need to persuade that the illness is 'real', but at the same time to present oneself as a moral and worthy person. Moreover, accounts can never be expected to provide consistent concepts of health, because they are tied up with other areas of life: illness is given meaning through its consequences for a particular person in a particular situation. The account cannot be assumed to follow some external logic, and the concepts are inseparable from the activity of accounting.

Lay concepts and behaviour

People's concepts and experience of health and illness do, of course, have some behavioural and clinical significance. While the initial suggestion in social psychology, medical anthropology and medical sociology, that lay and medical views were far apart and in need of reconciliation, may have been left behind, it is still true that their beliefs determine in part when and where someone seeks help for their illness, whether they 'co-operate' with treatment, and how they receive the information that they are given. Also, beliefs, especially about cause, will still have relevance to the way people act – their choices of lifestyle and responses to health promotion. It is to these ways in which health and illness are 'enacted' that the next chapter turns.

4
How is Health Enacted?

The interest of clinicians, public health, or policy-makers in these complex perceptions of what health and illness are relates, of course, to the fact that people's actions are affected – their recognition that they may be in need of medical help, their behaviour when they are ill, their health-protective or health-harming lifestyles, and their relationship with their doctors. This chapter, while focusing still on the sick or well individual, considers how people enact the states of being healthy or ill. What people say – the topic of the last chapter – and what they do may be different things. It is generally accepted that attitudes and beliefs, though they may have associations with actions, are rather poor predictors of them.

A somewhat outmoded term for this area of sociology is illness 'behaviour'. Quah (2001: 28) suggests that in fact three distinct terms have been used:

- *preventive behaviour*, or the activity undertaken for the purpose of preventing illness
- *illness behaviour*, or the activity undertaken by a person who is ill in order to define the illness and seek a solution, that is, the perception of symptoms and the decision to seek help
- *sick role behaviour*, or the formal response to symptoms, including the seeking of formal help and the subsequent action of the person as patient.

Preventive behaviour and health-promoting behaviour are also sometimes distinguished: preventive acts include the use of specific services such as immunization, dental care or breast self-examination, that is, health viewed within a model of not-diseased. Health-promoting acts, on the other hand, are lifestyle habits such as taking exercise or eating healthily, that is, health defined more positively and holistically.

The rise and fall of 'illness behaviour'

Perhaps the first impetus given to the study of health behaviour was the realization that most people, most of the time, are experiencing some symptom which they could call 'illness' if they wished. The perception of being in 'perfect' health in every system of the body is rare. Surveys presenting populations with symptom lists ('Have you, in the last fortnight, suffered from headache, foot problems, indigestion, backache, toothache, depression. . . .'), or the use of diaries, where people were asked to record every health-related event or sensation, showed clearly that few people could not identify themselves somewhere on the lists, or go through many days without a twinge of pain. Yet, obviously, not all this 'illness' is brought for professional attention. This recognition of the 'illness iceberg', and the fact that there was little, medically, to distinguish the symptoms brought to a doctor from those ignored, tolerated or self-treated, turned attention to illness behaviour. What determines the identification of bodily sensations as 'ill'?

In the early days of medical sociology, Mechanic (1968: 116) defined 'illness behaviour' as the way in which 'symptoms are differentially perceived, evaluated and acted upon (or not acted upon) by different kinds of people and in different social situations'. This became extended to include not only people's recognition of and reaction to symptoms, and their help-seeking, but also reactions to the illness itself and to treatment, and eventually all patterns of behaviour associated with health. With regard to the beginning of the 'illness career', Mechanic suggested ten relevant processes:

- visibility, recognizability or perceptual salience of the symptoms
- their perceived seriousness
- the extent to which they disrupt family, work and other social activities
- their frequency or persistence
- the tolerance threshold of those who are exposed to and evaluate them, including the self and others
- available information, knowledge and cultural assumptions and understandings
- psychological processes such as denial or fear
- other needs or motives competing with the response to illness
- competing possible interpretations of the symptoms
- availability of treatment resources, and the costs (monetary or other) of taking action.

The *health belief model* (HBM) (Rosenstock 1974) and its variants which had been employed to formalize these processes were much used, especially in psychology, to identify the factors that influence people to act 'healthily' or seek medical help. A great deal of effort was spent in devising and testing models of the stages of the transformation of perceived illness into disease or sickness. The HBM models decision-making according to two forms of motivation in dynamic interplay: predisposing factors and enabling factors. Assumed influences on the readiness to act include such things as concern about health matters in general, the perceived severity of the threat which is being presented by not acting, the perceived susceptibility to this harm, and the likelihood of the effectiveness of taking action. Enabling factors include personal characteristics such as age, structural factors such as the cost of the action, the facilities which are available, and social pressures to act. The first set of factors represent readiness to take the action, and the second determine whether it is actually taken.

Much effort was spent in refining models such as this about individual decision-making, and also in trying to characterize the groups in society who might differ in responses to illness. There was, for instance, classic work, particularly in the USA, mapping out 'illness behaviour' among different socio-economic groups. Why did the poor appear to define health differently, or be less able to follow medically approved pathways, or consult 'appropriately', than those who were not materially or educationally disadvantaged?

Models such as the HBM were criticized, however, because they seemed deterministic and abstracted from social settings. They predetermined what was to be included or excluded in the model and thus were seen as culturally biased. It was questioned whether these few dimensions could ever predict the variety of outcomes for different groups in different settings or do justice to the complexity of human experience.

All the factors of motivation and perceived benefits and barriers will depend on the characteristics of the person concerned, and will differ between groups of the population. Perceived seriousness of an infection, for instance, may depend on age, and the amount of threat depends not only on how a symptom is perceived as disease but also its functional importance: slight stiffness of the joints might represent extreme threat to a pianist while being barely noticeable to others. Cultural groups seem to respond to pain differently, and particularly in the USA, with its multicultural society, there were many classic studies in the 1950s and 1960s showing the variation in reaction to pain of Americans of different racial and cultural backgrounds. Occupational cultures (athletes, heavy manual workers) also shape responses to pain. It is suggested that the major source of 'cultural' variation such as this is socialization – the way in which people are taught, explicitly and implicitly, the values of their social group. The differing socialization of girls and boys has also been seen as relevant to responses to illness of men and women.

The definition of a symptom will also depend on circumstances and health experience. If an experience has once been defined and dealt with, a similar condition is likely to be so defined again. In an early American study, Koos (1954) said of a woman in 'Regionville':

> She talked about her own cold and about her husband's hernia, but was confused about what illness really meant. She was unconcerned about swollen ankles and shortness of breath and did not consider them reason for seeing a doctor. Her mother had had swollen ankles and shortness of breath for some years before she died, and had not seen a doctor.

An individual's perception of symptoms often depends to a considerable extent, of course, on the perception of others. Symptoms affect day-to-day behaviour, and have repercussions on those around. A complex of family lore may be brought to bear on the situation. In some cases, relatives may encourage a definition of illness; in others, they may deny that the symptom exists or that it can be defined as illness ('You're overworked . . . stressed . . . need a holiday'). For oneself, there is a common natural tendency to rationalize and normalize symptoms if it is at all possible. The possibility of normalization, and the form it takes, will depend on the pattern of life in a particular group. People who do heavy work may consider backache normal; people who work long hours may expect to be tired; many symptoms are unnecessarily ascribed to 'it's just old age'. If a symptom is not too disabling and a simple cause not in the category of illness can be found, it may be ignored.

An early study in South Wales, using family diaries, illustrated these processes of definition very clearly. Robinson (1971) asked the mothers of families to record, day by day, every symptom or health event experienced, the action taken, and comments on what the mother thought about it. These were graphic accounts of the build-up of stresses within a family, the manoeuvrings around the idea of illness, and the complexities of decision-making concerning what to do about it. There was the story, for instance, of a football injury a man sustained just before starting a new job, and all the reasons why it was impossible to consult about it, 'go sick', just at that time; or the diary of a mother at her wit's end with every member of the family recording daily symptoms – until something was done about the 'real' problem, one particular child who was referred to a specialist. At this point no further illnesses were reported for ten days and the family's health immediately 'improved'.

Person to patient: help-seeking behaviour

This leads to the next stage of the enactment of illness, or what Zola (1973) called the 'pathway from person to patient'. When and why are illnesses found to be appropriate for professional treatment? Even if there is agreement about what constitutes illness, there may be differences of opinion about the appropriate action. In *The Social System* (1951) Parsons had placed the behaviour of the possibly ill person within a theoretical framework by delineating a 'sick role'. This was one of the key points in the contract of rights, obligations and privileges between the ill person, their doctors and society. To gain the right to a 'sick role', to be recognized as legitimately ill, people must conform to the norms of this role. They must:

- want to get well
- seek professional advice and cooperate with it.

In return, they would receive associated privileges. They:

- may relinquish their normal activities and responsibilities
- will be regarded as being in need of care and be absolved of responsibility for their illness.

This was not meant as a description of what actually occurs, but as an ideal-type scenario describing a functional system. Nevertheless, criticisms of this theoretical approach spilled over into complaints that, empirically, it did not actually fit into experience. Chronic disease was particularly difficult to accommodate in this framework, since the patient may not expect to 'get well'. It described an unhelpfully passive patient who took no responsibility. Moreover, the study of the 'illness iceberg' showed that there were other means of dealing with illness besides seeking professional advice, including self-treatment, lay consultation and non-medical treatment. As Zola (1973: 679) noted:

> Virtually every day of our lives we are subject to a vast array of bodily discomforts. Only an infinitesimal amount of these get to a physician. Neither the mere presence nor the obviousness of symptoms, neither their medical serio usness nor objective discomfort, seems to differentiate those episodes which do and do not get professional treatment. In short, what then does convert a person to a patient? . . . 'something critical' must ordinarily happen to make an individual seek

help. Given the voluminous literature on delay in seeking medical aid for almost every conceivable disorder and treatment, we might well say that the statistical norm for any population is to delay (perhaps infinitely for many).

There must be particular points where the scales are tipped in favour of professional definition of the illness. The question becomes not why does the individual consult a doctor, but why does he or she consult *now*? Zola identified these 'triggers' to the decision to seek medical aid as:

• interpersonal crisis
• perceived interference with social or personal relations
• sanctioning by others
• perceived interference with work or physical activity
• temporalizing of symptomatology – the setting of external time criteria for the duration of symptoms or their recurrence.

Early literature on 'the decision to consult', based on an essentially 'medical' model, focused on the rationality or otherwise of decisions. The individually oriented studies of what actually happens in illness episodes showed, however, that what might be defined as rational depends on many factors outside the context of the illness – not simply the objective seriousness of the symptoms and the prognosis, but the importance of the prospective patient's engagements next week, the effect of being formally labelled as 'ill' upon a personal relationship or an employer, the whole practical structure of life. Rational decision-making requires full knowledge of probabilities of outcomes, something rarely available to the individual actor. Accounts of decisions to seek help are full of the continual processes of assessment and reassessment, definition and redefinition, which go on before action is taken and a doctor is consulted or not consulted.

Many studies show that stress is an important trigger to help-seeking. It may, of course, be that stress precipitates illness, or that illness is a cause of stress. Possibly, given that symptoms exist, it is stressful episodes which trigger the decision to do something about them. There is certainly evidence that an extra stress does often precede consultation for previously neglected symptoms. The decision often comes as the climax of a building-up of tension.

Moreover, the decision to seek help is rarely carried out in isolation. An early description of the process was that of the American sociologist Freidson:

> Indeed, the whole process of seeking help involves a network of potential consultants, from the intimate and informal confines of the nuclear family through successively more select, distant, authoritative laymen, until the 'professional' is reached. This network of consultants, which is part of the structure of the local lay community and which imposes form on the seeking of help, might be called the 'lay referral structure.' Taken together with the cultural understandings involved in the process, we may speak of it as the 'lay referral system.' (Freidson 1960: 377)

Modern health systems have developed this process beyond referral to, or from, family and acquaintances. Information is available in more and more sophisticated forms, and the availability of alternative therapies, or professions ancillary to medicine, is more and more institutionalized. The pathway to becoming a patient becomes easier in some ways, since accessibility of care is stressed as a policy objective in most modern medical systems. On the other hand, the distinction between person and patient becomes more complicated. This will be discussed in chapter 6.

Enacting the illness role

Mechanic (1968: 86) had stressed the positive control which people struggle to maintain over events around 'being ill':

> much of human activity and the activity surrounding illness can be accounted for within a framework which views such behaviour as aspects and reactions to situations where persons are actively struggling to control their environment and their life situation. Much of the behaviour of the patient [and, Mechanic added later, of the professionals dealing with them] in defining illness and responding to it can be explained in terms of his adaptive needs.

However, research and theory in the mid-twentieth century still focused on groups and cultures – this behaviour would be typical of this race or nationality rather than that, of women rather than men, of the poorly educated rather than the well-educated, and so on. Particularly, once the 'person' had become 'patient', the individual was regarded passively, as at best a collaborator or partner in his or her own treatment. The emphasis was on 'compliance' with the doctor's advice and attempts to explain non-compliance as irrational behaviour. Was it simply ignorance, requiring better education? Or the conflict of lay and scientific beliefs? Or tension between controlling doctors and their resentful patients, who tried by choosing their own path to retain some control? However, of more recent decades there has been a movement into realization that, while this body of work had some practical importance – for instance, in identifying and removing barriers to medical care or reasons connected with the structure of care for poor collaboration with doctors – it did not provide answers to the questions about how, and why, individual people acted as they did.

Concepts such as the sick role, the patient role – and even the doctor role – have been recognized as a product of a particular cultural phase, the supremacy of the biomedical model in which behaviour is seen as response to the biomedical state of disease. As Frank (1995: 11) noted:

> The ill person who plays out Parsons's sick role accepts having the particularity of his individual suffering reduced to medicine's general view. Modernity did not question this reduction because its benefits were immediate and its cost was not yet apparent. The colonization of experience was judged worth the cure, or the attempted cure. But illnesses have shifted from the acute to the chronic, and self-awareness has shifted. The post-colonial ill person, living with illness for the long term, wants her own suffering recognised in its individual particularity; 'reclaiming' is the relevant postmodern phrase.

In view of the complexity of lay ideas and responses to illness discussed in chapter 3, obviously the enacting of illness is much more than simply the question of understanding or not, and following or not, a doctor's instructions. Much of the literature of the 1970s and 1980s, and indeed some contemporary medical and pharmaceutical literature, relates to 'compliance', or whether the patient accepts the doctor's instructions or takes medications as prescribed, attempting to show how degree of adherence to the prescribed regimen is structured by, for instance, age or education. 'Non-compliance' has tended to be seen in terms of patient error, ignorance or misunderstanding. Actions which are not consistent with medical advice are seen as illogical or deviant, and patients are unhelpfully divided into only two categories: those who do and those who do not follow instructions. In general, studies have produced inconsistent or inconclusive results, with the only certain finding that the majority of patients do not take their drugs as prescribed.

Of more recent years, there has been considerable criticism of this body of work, both in medicine and in pharmacy. If compliance is defined as the extent to which the ill person's behaviour coincides with medical advice, this is seeing behaviour from the doctor's point of view rather than the patient's. It is widely found that it is difficult to divide patients simply into two categories, the compliant and the non-compliant: most are mixed, according to their reading of the circumstances. It has been suggested that 'adherence' is a preferable term, implying a more active, collaborative participation, though this still invokes a notion of 'correct' behaviour as a standard. The conventional perspective, it has been suggested, ignores the lay meanings of medications and procedures and their place in the context of the individual's life: non-adherence may be a perfectly rational response to a perceived lack of benefits from the treatment, undue side effects, or simply the greater importance of other issues in the patient's life. 'Concordance' is an alternative term popular in primary care, implying a course of action agreed upon in negotiation between doctor and patient, which is more likely to be followed than one simply imposed by the doctor.

Much of the understanding of how people may act in illness, including their adherence to treatment, comes from studies of groups suffering from particular chronic diseases, including especially diabetes, heart disease, asthma, hypertension and epilepsy. Such studies tend to find that, although many fail to conform to their prescribed regimens, they define this as self-regulation or control rather than non-compliance. The modification of medication has been shown to be used, for instance, explicitly to test the existence, diagnosis and progress of their illness, and to help in the management of everyday life. Over-the-counter medications have similarly been described as tools for diagnostic and control strategies.

Apart from this work specifically on adherence, and many descriptive studies of reaction to various diseases (and a growing genre of personal autobiographical accounts of life-threatening illness), there is a lack of study of how people enact their illness – how they actually behave – to match the wealth of discussion about how they perceive it and narrate it described in chapter 3. The field is certainly lacking any coherent theory to replace the rejected sick role or passive patient. There is a handful of exceptions: Radley and Green (1987), for instance, identified four different styles of adjustment to pain and chronic illness: accommodation, active-denial, secondary gain, and resignation. These are located on a four-way grid in which the self is either opposed to the illness or complementary to it, and social participation is either retained or lost. 'Accommodation', for instance, means that the self is complementary to the illness and participation is retained, and tends to occur where roles are more flexible and more choice is available about the presentation of the symptoms. 'Active-denial' involves opposition to the illness through increasing engagement in everyday activities. In 'resignation', the self is opposed to illness and social participation is lost.

Another theoretical model is provided by Frank. In illness, he suggests,

> people who have always *been* bodies have distinct problems *continuing* to be bodies, particularly continuing to be the same sorts of bodies they have been. The body's problems during illness are not new [but] illness requires new and more self-conscious solutions to these general problems. (Frank 1995: 28)

Four general problems of embodiment are proposed, each a problem of action: each has a range of possible responses. These produce four 'ideal typical' bodies in illness, and actual people, of course, present a mixture of these:

1 *The problem of control* The body is, it is suggested, lived along a continuum from predictability to contingency. Disease is itself a loss of predictability and 'causes further losses: incontinence, shortness of breath or memory, tremors and seizures, and all the other failures of the sick body'. Loss of control is stigmatizing, as Goffman (1967) pointed out, and stigma which is imposed by others on the ill represents general social ambivalence over what is happening. Various reactions can be enacted: 'passing' as normal, if possible, or regaining some control by the contemporarily approved method of 'coming out' or deliberately claiming the 'deviant' identity. Strategies vary as to what can be controlled, where, and how.

2 *The problem of body-relatedness* Bodies may be associated with or disassociated from: 'do I *have* a body, or *am* I a body?' Frank suggests that modern Western medicine, with its emphasis on images and machines, discourages body association, and this is one of the reasons for the growth in the popularity of alternative healers. In illness, however, the quality of association with one's body inevitably changes.

3 *The problem of other-relatedness* Other-relatedness as a problem of action pertains to 'how the shared condition of being bodies becomes a basis of empathic relations among living human beings.' Ill people are both wholly individual in their suffering and sharing it with others. The *monadic* body sees itself as essentially separate and alone; *dyadic* bodies exist for each other.

4 *The problem of desire* Frank expresses this as: what do I want, and how is it expressed for, with and through my body? Ill bodies may come to lack desire, may mean 'ceasing to think yourself desirable to yourself: the ill person fears he is no longer worth clean teeth and new shoes.' On the other hand, illness may provide 'permission' for new desires.

These four 'problems' set up a fourfold typology of the way in which people act out their illness. The *disciplined* body defines itself primarily in actions of self-regimentation, and its most important problems of action are those of control. It seeks to restore predictability through treatment, displays monadic self-enclosure, disassociates from a body that becomes 'it', and may lose desire. The *mirroring* body also seeks predictability, but of appearance rather than function, and mirrors its desires on others who are its audience or on popular culture. The *dominating* body assumes contingency but does not accept it. It is disassociated from self, lacks desire and turns on others. Frank notes that this is an enactment of illness which rarely appears in illness 'narratives', but is nevertheless common, if only for part of the time. The *communicative* body is an idealized type: it is fully accepting of contingency and associated with itself; the ill body 'constructs its humanity in relation to other bodies.' Frank emphasizes that these four types cannot be either mutually exclusive or exhaustive, and any actual body represents a layering of types. Nevertheless they provide a model for readings of how people act out an illness.

These remain, however, unusual examples of contemporary theorizing about illness behaviour.

Behaving 'healthily'

The same is not true of *health* behaviour. The questions here are: What place do considerations of health have in the conduct of people's lives? What do they perceive as acting 'healthily' and why do they engage – or not – in these activities? Who takes advantage of all the preventive services that may be available, and why do some refuse them? How do people relate to the healthy body? In particular, how do more holistic concepts of health affect lifestyles and general courses of action, not simply responses to illness? The fact that there is more interest in theory here may perhaps represent some of the effects of the transition from the 'medical' to the 'social' model of health. Illness behaviour, even from the patient's point of view, had still been seen as a coda to the medical model, demonstrating no more than ways in which that model might be revised. *Health* behaviour, on the other hand, represents the social model, and there is more interest in theorizing it.

The study of health behaviour, no less than illness behaviour, did, however, begin with a medical model. In early work, social maladjustment – of which patterns of health-related behaviour could be seen as a part – was viewed primarily as a function of personality, in part the product of socialization. Early interest was largely in explaining, and knowing perhaps how to change, the attitudes of those who did not appear to value their health, or behave responsibly, or use the preventive services offered. In the 1960s and 1970s there was much interest in explaining the health behaviour of the socially deprived as part of a 'subculture of poverty', characterized by marginality, a low level of social organization, helplessness, dependence, ignorance and inferiority. Apathy and fatalism, it was suggested, might explain the underuse by the poor of preventive medicine in the USA and the low value which appeared to be placed upon the maintenance of health. This subculture was alienated from the values of modern medicine, and preventive behaviour in particular required an orientation towards the future, an exercise of 'deferred gratification', which was incompatible with fatalism. Medical professionals and their middle-class patients shared a rational or scientific approach to health, from which deprived subcultures were excluded.

In subsequent decades, this subcultural model was criticized and gave way to one which emphasized rather the practical barriers to 'healthy' behaviour, and the way in which preventive health care was offered. 'Healthy' behaviour was conventionally defined primarily in terms of smoking, diet, exercise habits, and alcohol or other drug consumption. A great deal of work was devoted to demonstrating that, though knowledge and attitudes to health are undoubtedly relevant, patterns for each of these owe more to the social environment and social pressures and to external factors such as the constraints of poverty, conditions under which lives are led, society's structures of control, and commercial pressures or cultural fashions.

Each of the health 'habits' is of course an immense topic in itself, in behavioural, psychological and physiological science. Some very broad general conclusions can be suggested, relevant to the present discussion. Each of the conventionally identified health behaviours is, of course, very clearly associated with health. They (or any other constellation of behaviours which could be targeted) do not necessarily, however, cohere into a consistent pattern of 'healthy behaviour'. Different groups of populations are typically subject to different patterns of 'behavioural risk factors'. Moreover, the enacting of these behaviours, or their avoidance (in a healthy person), often has little to do with concepts of health. Young men may find other rewards in sporting exercise, for instance, or people may have moral rather than health-related attitudes towards alcohol or drug use. Some people may eschew smoking because they believe it will harm their health, or adopt a particular diet for health reasons, but there are many other factors in tastes, social circumstances and social pressures for these actions that have nothing to do with health. Unhealthy behaviour, in real lives, may have rational causes. Moreover, while some healthy behaviour patterns are the product of better knowledge and education, the association is not necessarily clear-cut. In the population survey referred to earlier in connection with health beliefs (Blaxter 1990), almost 100 per cent identified smoking as a cause of disease, with little difference between smokers and non-smokers. Among those whose measured body mass index fell into the 'obese' category, 35 per cent said that overweight was a cause of heart disease, compared with 21 per cent of those who were not themselves overweight. It was suggested that the basic lessons of health promotion had been almost entirely accepted, and those who behaved 'unhealthily' were as likely – if not more likely – to be aware of the dangers. In general discussions about their own health, they might of course be given to finding excuses for their own lifestyles or complex causes for their own diseases. They were rarely, however, ignorant of the well-publicized effects of smoking, diet or exercise.

Structure/agency: health as cultural consumption

Although attempts to categorize individuals simply as displaying 'internal' or 'external' orientations in the way they behave in relation to health may now be old-fashioned, contemporary discussion still very much emphasizes the 'structure/agency' question, or the ancient debate about the extent to which people can exercise individuality and free will or are subject to various kinds of constraint. Can individuals act healthily in a wholly voluntary manner, or do the social structures in which they live or social norms and values limit what is possible or likely? To what extent do people choose unhealthy habits, and to what extent are they imposed upon them? The classic sociologist Max Weber provided a theoretical background for these discussions. He identified two concepts: life conduct and life chances. Conduct represents agency or choice, the way in which people voluntarily act. Chances represent class position, the boundaries within which people act, according to their social situation. The interplay of these is a dominant theme because of its practical and political interest in the fields of health promotion and health inequalities.

The commodification of health, emphasizing the range of dietary, leisure, slimming, body maintenance and decoration products which modern commerce and culture provide, and popular media publicize, is a popular theme of contemporary thinking about health. Cosmetic surgery, the promotion of the young and fit body as a fashionable ideal, aggressive marketing of health as a product in the form of 'healthy' foods, supplements or activities, the evidence of pathologies such as anorexia or compulsive exercise – all these are indicted as 'cultural' distortions of the concept of health which it is difficult for the individual to escape. This emphasis on the healthy body and the individual's right and duty to cherish it fits, of course, with the individualistic 'lifestyle' approach of much contemporary public health policy. Health-relevant habits are not seen in isolation but as part of lifestyles: the holistic idea of lifestyle – become, popularly, a term meaning simply consumption – has replaced the attention paid to discrete actions such as eating this or that, consulting a doctor or not, or accepting immunization or not.

Crawford (1984) was one of the earliest and most illuminating writers on this question of how people see themselves as enacting health in a consumer society. Health can be acted out in terms of self-control, self-discipline and willpower, because lifestyle 'has become life-denying, with the consumption of unhealthy products, the pursuit of high-risk activities, the sedentary nature of modern life.' Health maintenance must be disciplined within a moral discourse, a shared cultural value of what it means to be a moral person. Crawford argues that we internalize the mandate for control:

> Our bodies, 'the ultimate metaphor', refract the general mood. We cut out the fat, tighten our belts, build resistance, and extend our endurance. Subject to forces that lie beyond individual control, we attempt to control what is within our grasp. Whatever practical reasons and concerns lead us to discipline our bodies in the name of health or fitness, the ritualized response to economic crisis finds in health and fitness a compatible symbolic field. (Crawford 1984: 148)

But there are other forces impelling towards release, the imperative to indulge:

> Rather than deny the self, the premise is instant contentment. Social institutions are mobilized to produce a personality structure compatible with consumption. Whereas production requires a structuring of time to the industrial clock, consumption must reorganize non-working time into 'leisure' and 'lifestyle' – a transformation into time available for buying and using an endless array of products. The sign of our culture, projected on bill-boards and television screens, is unambiguous: the 'good life' means a life of consumption. (Crawford 1984: 141)

Theorizing health as consumption owes much to the work of the French sociologist Bourdieu, who extended analysis to the explanation of class and group differences in health behaviour. Bourdieu focused on how the practices of individuals – their everyday habits – are influenced by the structure of their social world and, in turn, create that structure. Individual practices are connected to culture and structure, and ultimately to power, through the concept of *habitus*. Habitus is defined as the ensemble of dispositions by which actions and attitudes in the everyday world are habituated and taken for granted, because they are embodied. A framework of perceptions, formed through experience, socialization and class circumstances, predisposes the individual towards particular behaviour. Thus behavioural choices are typically in keeping with the norms of a group or social class, and the habitus imposes boundaries on the probable forms of action.

Bourdieu (1984) demonstrated, for instance, that cultural consumption in food habits and in sports in France was shaped by class-related norms of behaviour, established through group interaction and internalized, so that both internal and external constraints put boundaries on what was possible. The tastes of workers, within a working-class habitus, take forms which distinguish them from the middle class, who have different tastes. Tastes are ways in which people establish social superiority and express relationships of dominance. The relevance of these ideas in the context of health is that behaviours, even those which might seem most closely related to health, may have powerful springs which arise elsewhere.

Structure/agency: health as self-governance

Health as consumption emphasizes choice, even if culturally constrained. A related strand of theory and discussion is health as 'personal body projects', as individualized self-control in the contemporary 'surveillance society'.

The French philosopher and historian Michel Foucault (1973, 1977) was influential in describing a particularly modern form of governmental power, based on the extension of the 'medical gaze' from individual bodies to the surveillance of populations, requiring individuals to govern themselves, and promoting self-control, responsibility, rationality and self-knowledge. This is not seen, necessarily, as repressing the liberty of the individual. People become more than docile and passive objects, since preventive health programmes make them a part of their own health management.

It is relevant that the second half of the twentieth century saw the shift from predominantly acute, often infectious, conditions to chronic diseases such as cancer, diabetes or heart disease. The movement from treatment to surveillance, from curing to caring, is in part a consequence. If cure is not an appropriate concept then medicine must, instead, consider prevention and management. Alternative and complementary therapies are increasingly used by both patients and doctors. People are encouraged to monitor their own health status. Disease is now placed in a wider time-framework: we look to the future, to risk and probabilities of ill health. Illness symptoms may be not simply problems of themselves, but risk factors associated with other conditions. Characteristics acquired at birth, through genetic inheritance or otherwise, may not manifest themselves as illness but may be seen as disease-in-waiting. The incorporation of the social into the medical model means that risk factors are not restricted to the physical: behaviours are risk factors, and indeed activities like smoking are seen almost as diseases of themselves.

As Armstrong (1993: 65) notes, the boundary between the healthy person and the patient becomes problematic:

> The dream of the new medicine has reformed the relationship between health and illness. No longer polar opposites within a binary classification, they have become inextricably linked within a great continuum of health. On the one hand health is contained in illness; the disabled, the chronically sick, the dying and the diseased can promote their health by appropriate health behaviour, enabling reactions and successful coping. Equally the germ of illness is now contained in health. Health has become a temporal trajectory containing the seeds of illness which, nevertheless, can be countered by preventive action, health promotion, healthy living, and healthy lifestyles.

These personal body projects, the new 'inward gaze', aim at what Chrysanthou (2002: 472) has called 'Somatopia', the perfect, imperishable body. The well and the ill are no longer clearly distinguished:

> In Somatopia, a third kingdom comes into existence: the Kingdom of the in-between. We are all at some time dwellers in the in-between, taking our place alongside hypochondriacs, the worried well, the worried-and-maybe-not-well, and the not-worried-but-think-maybe-they-ought-to-be. In Somatopia, where the ideology of healthism is wide-spread, and the rituals of self-surveillance are scrupulously observed, the Kingdom of the in-between is routinely crowded.

In the immensely complex network of modern medical and community care, the patients themselves become 'producers' of health through their health-protecting and -enhancing action. Illness moves out from the body to 'problems of coping and adjustment, and medical strategies shift from the pronouncements of experts towards "informed choice", and non-directive counselling' (Armstrong 1993: 66).

At the same time, political agendas rise, their acceptability fed by some general disillusion with medicine. As Crawford (1977) noted, the placing of responsibility on the individual – 'You are dangerous to your health' – can be a political ideology which results in blaming the victim for their own ill health. People are instructed to be individually responsible at a time when they are becoming less capable, as individuals, to control the features in their environment which harm their health. If faith in medicine is eroded by the non-appearance of the 'magic bullet' and the fear of over-reliance on technology – and, it must be added, if societies find the cost of medicine difficult to sustain – then prevention, and individual responsibility, are obviously attractive answers. The concept of health itself changes.

5
How is Health Related to Social Systems?

The individuals whose ideas of health and experiences of illness were the subject of the last two chapters do not, of course, live in isolation. The way in which a society is organized, its resources and their distribution, has a profound effect on the individuals within it.

> Everywhere and in all periods, it is the individual who is sick, but he is sick in the eyes of his society, in relation to it, and in keeping with the modalities fixed by it. The language of the sick . . . takes place within the language expressing the relations between the individual and society. (Herzlich and Pierret 1987: xi)

Health becomes a political and ethical issue.

Most of the significant differences in health between countries, populations, and groups within countries are not genetic or in any other sense biologically inevitable. They are bound up with that society, its particular place and time, its politics and organization. At the same time, the health of populations has consequences for the prosperity of their societies: for instance, in developing countries, disease can be an obstacle to economic progress. Society has a duty to consider the health of its populations which is both utilitarian and ethical. During the era of the Industrial Revolution in the West, the British pioneer of public health Edwin Chadwick brought to the attention of legislators that the economic cost of the ill health of the poor, taking into account the support of widows and children, was great, but the damage to society went beyond the financial cost. Health is part of a society's capital, and at the same time the health of the population is one of society's responsibilities. The relationship is a reciprocal one.

A functional relationship

Two of the most influential founding theorists on the relationship of health to society were Durkheim and Parsons, holding models of society which are called functionalist. The ideas of structural functionalism were an attempt to account for social activity by referring to its consequences for society as a whole, and to show how patterns of behaviours and institutions are created in ways which contribute to the maintenance of a social system.

The French sociologist Emile Durkheim emphasized the importance of societal structures, norms and processes – things which were outside individuals but integrated them into the larger society. Religion, for instance, was best understood as contributing to the integration and stability of society. In *Rules of Sociological Method* (1985) he argued that social facts are representations of society in people's minds: they are ways of thinking and feeling, cultural and moral beliefs, religious practices and social norms of behaviour. They represent the social solidarity and collective consciousness that bind societies or groups together. In *Suicide, a Study in Sociology* (1987) he used the example of suicide, developing a typology of three major types of suicide: egoistic, where the individual was detached from society; anomic, due to a state of normlessness; and altruistic, a positive and purposive choice. The prevalence of the individual act of taking one's own life was determined by ties in the community or society.

The concept of *anomie*, in particular, proved of lasting importance in theories about health and society. Durkheim argued that human well-being depends on wants being proportionate to the means available by which they might be filled. Societies cope with the problem of limitless desires, as a fact of human nature, and necessarily limited resources by imposing a framework of expectations about accepted conduct which 'permits' only those goals which have some chance of attainment. When, or if, this framework breaks down, goals again outrun means and individuals experience the state of anomie or normlessness, which may lead to suicide. Later researchers and theorists have extended this to consider general effects on health.

Talcott Parsons, influenced by Durkheim and by Max Weber, as well as by early psychoanalytical theory, also emphasized value consensus, social order, stability and functional processes. He saw the social order as fragile and always in danger of breaking apart. How do societies (for most of the time) persist in a stable fashion? The function of roles and institutions, the ways in which any society is ordered, is to maintain this stability – not necessarily by policing, but by people's internalized self-control.

In the major work *The Social System* (1951) a synthesis was attempted between the analysis of individual action and the analysis of large-scale social systems. The concept that bridges them is called the 'pattern variables' which structure any system of interaction. These represent the alternative choices which underlie people's behaviour:

- *universalism versus particularism*, or the way in which people relate to each other on the basis of general criteria, or alternatively on criteria specific to the individual concerned
- *performance versus ascription*, or whether people relate to each other on the basis of what they do and achieve or on the basis of qualities ascribed to them
- *specificity versus diffuseness*, or whether relationships are for a specific purpose or are general, across different areas of life
- *neutrality versus affectivity*, or whether people relate to one another in a detached and objective way, or with the engagement of emotions.

These represent norms and values which are critical, because they regulate how people behave and make interactions predictable, rather than idiosyncratic and random, so that social life is possible.

Systems, it was argued, have needs – both those imposed by the environment and those which the system's own nature require – which have to be met. Using the medical profession as the model for organizations based on professionalism and a service orientation, Parsons analysed the duties and the reciprocal entitlements of the patient and the doctor. For the doctor, the first of each of the 'pattern variables' was appropriate – universalism, performance, specificity and affective neutrality. The analysis of the 'sick role' has already been discussed. It is more than simply a theory of individual behaviour, however: Parsons is describing the key points of the contract involving rights, privileges and obligations which would identify medicine as functional in sustaining equilibrium in society and maintaining social order.

That it is possible for ill health to harm the social order, if only by reducing the capacities of a society's population, is obvious. It is equally obvious that it is the profession of medicine that is given, to a large extent, the duty of 'policing' as well as the duty of curing. The specific 'ideal type' details of the relationship which Parsons devised have, however, often been misinterpreted in later eras. They are not descriptive – 'this is how it is' – nor even normative – 'this is how patients and doctors ought to behave' – but theoretical: *if* the function of institutions is to maintain social stability, then these are the rules which are necessarily followed in the case of medicine.

Responses to functionalism

However, structural functionalism was short-lived as a leading theoretical paradigm in the study of health and society, losing influence in the 1960s and 1970s, for more important reasons than these quibbles about the 'sick role'.

The rise of symbolic interactionism, described in chapter 2, was influential. If social life is seen as produced by interacting agents constructing their behaviour on the basis of their own interpretations of situations, if institutions are created by reciprocal processes, then this is not compatible with a functionalist view which appears to relegate individuals to very passive roles. Moreover, the emphasis of functionalism on equilibrium and consensus seemed to favour the status quo and the dominance of the powerful. Particularly, it was found inadequate to explain change. Conflict theory, with its roots in Marx, maintains that society is not held together by shared norms and values: these are imposed by economically dominant groups. Marx held that people act upon the external world by means of 'labour' and the production of material objects: this is essentially a social process and has to be seen within given historical structures. Within the twentieth-century capitalist system, profit is achieved at the expense of those who provide labour, and, though the rapid growth of capital may increase the income of the worker, at the same time it increases the power of capital. Risks to health and longevity are graded by social status, and it follows that the cures for ill health lie in change in the social structure rather than change in the individual. Weber added that social differences are based not only on economic factors, on relationship to the 'means of production', but also on status and other forms of influence. Conflict theory turned attention, especially, to the sources of ill health in the economic environment and the competing interests in the organization of health care.

Medicine and society

Thus for some decades one of the major preoccupations of commentary and theory was the relationship of the profession of medicine with society, which is not necessarily the same thing as *health* and society. The institution and practice of medicine must obviously have relevance, however. In the later decades of the twentieth century the pre-eminence of medicine as a powerful grouping in society, combined with some disillusion about the actual effects or the possible longer-term consequences of high-technology medicine, led to an emphasis on a degree of conflict between the interests of patient and doctor, and on medicine as an 'institution of social control'. In the 1970s Illich, in particular, promulgated the idea that society was becoming increasingly medicalized. Doctors were becoming the new priesthood. Modern medicine was creating overdependence on technical fixes, with more and more areas of life subject to medical jurisdiction. Authors such as Navarro went further, emphasizing the role of the medical profession as the agent of the state. In a seminal essay, Zola analysed the increasing pervasiveness of medicine in terms of (1) the expansion of areas of life to which medicine was deemed to be relevant, (2) absolute control over certain technical procedures, (3) access to various 'intimate' areas of life, and (4) the expansion of medical involvement into ethical issues of the 'good' life. Medicine was, he suggested,

> becoming a major institution of social control, nudging aside, if not incorporating, the more traditional institutions of religion and law. It is becoming the new repository of truth, the place where absolute and often final judgements are made by supposedly morally neutral and objective experts. And these judgements are made, not in the name of virtue or legitimacy, but in the name of health. Moreover, this is not occurring through the political power physicians hold or can influence, but is largely an insidious and often undramatic phenomenon accomplished by 'medicalizing' much of daily living, by making medicine and the labels 'healthy' and 'ill' *relevant* to an ever increasing part of human existence. (Zola 1975: 170)

In the 1960s Foucault had written in *The Birth of the Clinic* on the way in which the new regime of the 'liberation of the insane, abolition of constraint' in the late eighteenth century was not truly liberation, for new forms of moral constraint, pervading more areas of life, were being applied. Increasingly, various institutions – not only hospitals, but prisons, schools – adopted a form of surveillance over their populations, which Foucault described as 'panopticism'. This all-seeing gaze is not simply an instrument of control. It actually constructs society's view of what it surveys. As Zola (1975: 500) said:

> C. S. Lewis warned more than a quarter of a century ago that 'man's power over Nature is really the power of some men over other men, with Nature as their instrument'. The same

could be said regarding man's power over health and illness. For the labels health and illness are remarkable 'depoliticizers' of an issue. By locating the source and the treatment of problems in an individual, other levels of intervention are effectively closed. By the very acceptance of a specific behaviour as an 'illness' and the definition of illness as an undesirable state the issue becomes not *whether* to deal with a particular problem but *how* and *when*. Thus, the debate over homosexuality, drugs, abortion, becomes focussed on the degree of sickness attached to the phenomenon in question or the extent of health risk involved. And the more principled, more perplexing, or even moral issue of *what* freedom should an individual have over his/her own body is shunted aside.

It is clinical knowledge which gives medicine power and authority. Foucault noted how 'becoming a patient' meant becoming vulnerable, a diminution of social and political status. The doctor develops a discourse which collapses speech (*parole*) and observation (*surveillance*) into one action, the gaze (*regard*): an act of objectification. He also described the 'medicine of the species' (diagnosis and treatment of disease, which makes the body an object for observation and treatment by the medical profession) and 'medicine of social spaces' (prevention, which makes public health subject to regulation by the state).

Armstrong (1993) has written of how, during the twentieth century, the main change in the nature of the 'clinical gaze' was the extension of surveillance from the interior of the body, the individual anatomy, to relationships or the social body. For instance, TB, previously a disease of individual bodies in disadvantaged environments, became a disease of contact. Nineteenth-century public health had been concerned with sanitation, with the dangers of the environment. With the rise of surveillance medicine, the focus of epidemiology began to shift from the environment to the mode of transmission between people. At the same time the 'atlas' which Foucault described as codifying and interpreting the body in the late eighteenth century becomes a new way of seeing it:

> The atlas is therefore a means of interpreting the body, of seeing its form and nature and establishing its reality. The modern body of the patient, which has become the unques-

tioned object of clinical practice, is a product of the exercise of those same clinical techniques. The clinical gaze, encompassing all the techniques, languages and assumptions of modern medicine, establishes by its authority and penetration an observable and analysable space in which is crystallised that apparently solid figure of the discrete human body. (Armstrong 1993: 56)

With the socio-medical survey as its tool, it became possible for public health to collate and assess population information, and define the 'normal' in terms of the average, using standardized indicators of mental and physical health (Armstrong 1995). More and more attributes of the individual, and ever-widening areas of human life, could be brought into the net of surveillance.

Health, economic development and social organization

Health and society do not interact only through the professions of public health and clinical medicine. A separate strand of theory relates to the relationship of economic development to health. This turns attention from the possibly oppressive effects of the systems and science of medicine to its obviously positive successes, together with economic development, in prolonging human lives.

For comparison over time or between different nations, average years of life expectancy is the most common measure, since all the ways in which illness might be measured or healthiness compared are so affected by cultural and system differences. Obviously, in the long term the health status of populations increases with economic development. That life expectancy at birth differs between regions of the world needs no emphasis: some figures are shown in table 5.1. This is health defined in the simplest terms, and economic development shown to affect health in the starkest way.

In the developed world, one of the most striking features of population health is that, in general, life expectancy continues to improve from one generation to the next. In 1900, the UK expectancy of life at birth of men was forty-four

Table 5.1   Years of life expectancy at birth, 1998

	Women	Men
Sub-Saharan Africa	51.0	48.4
India	57.1	57.9
'Established market economies' of developed world	80.5	73.4

years, in 1950–52 sixty-six years, and in 1991–3 almost seventy-four years. Now two or three years are added to life expectancy at birth with each decade that passes. It is not that old people live longer, but that more people live to be old, since death rates in infancy are particularly reduced. As Wilkinson (1996) notes, for the bulk of the population, the stranglehold on health of the absolute standard of living has been overcome. A rapid and sustained rise in living standards dates back to at least the middle of the nineteenth century. Wilkinson goes on to point out, however, that, though the curve relating the average life expectancy of different countries to their gross national product per capita (or income per capita) is very steep at low levels of income, it becomes flatter, in each historical period, as standards of living rise (see fig. 5.1). This is not because some absolute biological limit to life expectancy is being reached, since each stage of development shifts the life expectancy curve upwards. It does suggest, however, in any given period, 'the attainment among the majority of the population of a minimum real material standard of living, above which further increases in personal subsistence no longer provide the key to further increases in health.'

Some of the explanations for the associations between development and health are obvious: not only this 'real material standard of living', but the changing of disease patterns, especially the relative disappearance of infectious disease, the advances of public health and hygiene, and also the non-material benefits – education, for instance – associated with economic development. How much is due to the advances of medical science or the universal availability of modern medicine is problematic. McKeown et al. (1975), notably,

Life expectancy (years)

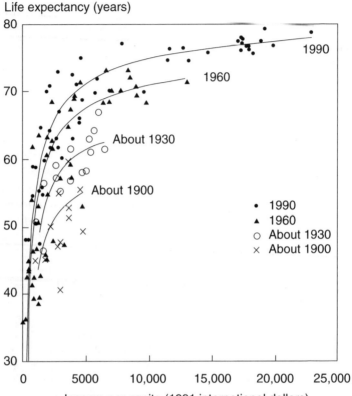

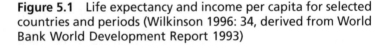

Figure 5.1 Life expectancy and income per capita for selected countries and periods (Wilkinson 1996: 34, derived from World Bank World Development Report 1993)

pointed out that the vast bulk of the decline in mortality from infectious disease came before the relevant advances of medicine – immunization, or effective forms of treatment – and suggested that increases in the standard of living, especially in housing and nutrition, must take the greatest credit for longer life. More recently, however, it has been pointed out that the thesis that medical science is not responsible for advances in population health is not necessarily always true: there are examples where decreases in death rates can be shown to be the effect of specific medical advances.

What is clear, however, is that, once a certain stage of development has been reached, systems of medicine – the proportion of gross national product spent on doctors and hospitals, for instance, or the way in which medical care is organized – are not very relevant to any differences between nations in the longevity of their populations.

The downside of economic development

Economic development obviously does bring with it benefits. On the other hand, the way in which it brings particular forms of harm to health is another of the major streams of thinking and research in modern times. Life expectancy is, of course, only one measure of health. Longer life means a greater likelihood of degenerative disease, so that the actual *experience* of ill health may in fact increase.

Because industrialization has been, historically, associated with development and with rising standards of living, epidemiologists and historians have studied particularly who gained and who lost in the process of industrialization, and how some of its obvious health-harming effects were distributed. There is some evidence that, in the United States in the mid-nineteenth century, even life expectancy declined and attained height – a standard indicator of the health of populations, within genetic limits – deteriorated. Suggested explanations were the easier spread of disease, and the emergence of cycles of prosperity and slump. During the early and mid-nineteenth century in the UK, deterioration in health was ascribed to urbanization and the deprivations of the urban poor. In 1842 Edwin Chadwick reported on *The Sanitary Conditions of the Labouring Population of Great Britain*, documenting their disadvantaged health and noting:

> We have seen that there are whole streets of houses, composing some of the wynds of Glasgow and Edinburgh, and great numbers of the courts in London, and the older towns in England, in which the condition of every inhabited room, and the physical condition of the inmates, is even more horrible than the worst of the dungeons that [prison reformer] Howard ever visited . . .

The health effects were unknown, or until then at least unacknowledged and unrecorded:

> The statements of the condition of considerable proportions of the labouring population of the towns into which the present inquiries have been carried have been received with surprise by persons of the wealthier classes living in the immediate vicinity, to whom the facts were as strange as if they related to foreigners or the natives of an unknown country. When Dr Arnott with myself and others were examining the abodes of the poorest classes in Glasgow and Edinburgh, we were regarded with astonishment; and it was frequently declared by the inmates, that they had never for many years witnessed the approach or the presence of persons of that condition near them.

A new perception of ill health as closely associated with poverty was being promulgated. Engels wrote on *The Condition of the Working Classes in England*, and half a century later in 1901 the social reformer Rowntree studied the city of York and noted the 'terrible waste of life' in the poorer areas, where more than a quarter of children died in their first year. Similar declines in the economic circumstances of groups of the population, with effects on health, are known for France, the Netherlands and other European countries.

This is health harm as a by-product of industrialization. More generally, it is argued that, in capitalist modes of operation, the health needs of the population will inevitably at some times come into conflict with the requirements of the capitalist system. In contemporary times, this strand of explanation is represented by the examination of historical trends, associating population health with particular periods of economic depression. At the level of individuals within a society, there is study of the effect of unemployment, local recession or economic uncertainty. In the UK, prospective studies of workplaces threatened with change, or workers becoming unemployed, have shown clear evidence of the way in which health is likely to deteriorate – whether through material hardship, changes in behaviour or psychosocial effects.

An associated topic of research and discussion is whether a society's welfare systems can provide effective buffers, with effects on health, against national, local or personal economic failure. It has sometimes been suggested that the better health of the Nordic states (as measured by longevity), compared with other countries at the same stage of development, can be ascribed to their well-developed institutional arrangements, including social benefits and welfare services. Research on a recent period of recession suggested that within each country the prevalence of ill health remained at similar levels, and the welfare services (which, though cut during the recession, broadly remained) may have acted as a buffer against the structural pressures (Lahelma et al. 2002).

That economic and political developments do have clear effects on population health has been demonstrated particularly by the recent history of the former Soviet Union and the countries of the former communist bloc (McKee 2001). These underwent extreme social and economic shock, inflation, unemployment, stress and insecurity, and experienced actual increases in mortality, though in some countries these have to some extent reversed. However, especially in Russia and the European countries of the former Soviet Union, a long-lasting health crisis appears to have resulted. In 1995 mortality rates in Russia among men were four times those in Western Europe, though there has been some more recent improvement. Various immediate causes have been discussed – environmental degradation, crime and violence, alcohol consumption, growing economic inequality – but in general terms this is seen as one of the clearest examples of the relationships between health and the economic organization of societies.

The concept of inequality in health

A basic corollary of the politico-economic view of the relationship of health to social structure is that the nature of the labour process in capitalism necessarily creates inequalities between sections of the population. 'Inequality' in health, in terms of comparing social groups within societies, has been one of the most active areas of research and discussion in the Western world for some three or four decades. Not only is this debate important for the understanding of health and society: it also reflects back upon some of the issues surrounding the concept of health itself.

What 'inequality' means in this context requires some consideration. Obviously, simple equality in health is impossible of attainment: differences in health, associated with genetic inheritance, gender, geography and pure chance (and of course age), are part of the human condition. Are we saying simply that people differ? Surveys of the views of ordinary people about health inequalities have tended to demonstrate a sturdy doubt about any structured relationship between social position and health: we are all individuals, and must all die, and

> I couldn't think it makes any difference myself. I mean, it's like people with money, they get the same illnesses as we get. So I shouldn't think it would make any difference whether you are skilled or unskilled. (working-class woman, quoted by Calnan 1987)

Or does inequality in health mean simply that there is inequality in all the things in life which might sustain health – food, living environments, medical care – and that the issue is only one of the extent of extreme economic deprivation? The evidence for a continuous gradient in health from the least to the most advantaged has been taken as meaning that inequality is more than this.

In effect, the term 'inequality in health' has come to mean a special sort of difference, in the context of social epidemiology and health policy. It can be defined as that difference in health between individuals or groups which is:

- *socially determined*, that is, due not to biological but to social factors. There are typical health differences between racial groups, for instance, which are biologically determined: they are not necessarily inequalities, though there may be other dimensions of race which are.
- *felt to be unjust*, inequitable or immoral: there are some typical differences in social groups which are viewed as their own choice, and not necessarily unjust. Inequalities tend always to have a moral dimension, but what is felt to be unfair is relative and susceptible to change.

• *held not to be inevitable*, that is, they could, within current technologies and knowledge, be alleviated. Thus, as technology advances, 'inequalities' become differently defined. As their cause is uncovered and cure or avoidance become possible, so they become not acts of God but human inequalities.

Thus the concept of inequality in health in Western societies is obviously a highly constructed one, depending on the social organization of societies, on ethical positions, and on the progress of science. It is obviously much more than equity of health-service provision, since, even if health-service supply were the crucial determinant of good health, equal services might result in very unequal health. 'Equity of provision for equal need' is a common way in which policy attempts to find a services-relevant description, but even this does not, of course, guarantee the abolition of inequalities in health. The measurement of inequalities in health is as problematic as the measures of 'health' itself considered in chapter l, with added layers of complexity caused by the need to define the social characteristics of the groups being compared.

The measure which is most often used, for whole populations, for the purposes of comparison over time or between nations, is rates of death, or life expectancy. The inequalities field has perhaps been responsible for putting a great emphasis on this as a measure of health. Age at death is not the only measure of health, however. As noted in chapter 1, mortality rates inevitably relate to causes in the past, and can only be measured retrospectively. Life expectancy at birth and life expectancy at, say, age sixty-five may be differently patterned, depending – for instance – on the importance in any specific group or society of infant deaths. Longevity may imply greater incapacity and dependence overall. For these reasons, 'years of *healthy* life', or 'potential years of life lost (PYLL) before the age of seventy' are measures which are used, the latter because investigating the causes of premature mortality may point to specific areas of intervention.

Inequalities may be measured in relative or in absolute terms – that is, as (for instance) the *ratio* of death rates in the 'lowest' group to those in the 'highest', or in terms of simple *difference* in years or life expectancy between the two groups. A nation with low mortality rates – Sweden has been noted as an example – may appear to have large inequalities if the relative method is used.

Other measures present other problems. Measures of illness, whether in the form of symptoms perceived or of judgements about one's own health, offer difficulties of cultural and individual differences, comparability and subjectivity. Statistics of diagnosed disease escape some of this, but are very dependent on perhaps different medical systems for identification. Measures based on function or physical ability raise the question: function for what?

It must be noted that, world-wide, there are considerable differences in perspective. In low-income countries, the extent of poor health among swathes of the population may have very obvious material causes of a lack of services and the basic necessities of life. The urgent questions may clearly be the economic and political ones of the extent and distribution of resources. A strong emphasis on equality of access to health care – not the same as equality in *health* – is also found among some of the wealthiest nations, such as the United States, with largely privatized health systems. Some countries such as America and Australia with large and disadvantaged ethnic or indigenous groups in their populations may also be particularly concerned with the 'inequality' of the health of different races.

In the UK and most of Western Europe, however, access to health services is relatively universal, and there is a tradition of agreement with the thesis of McKeown that, after a certain stage of economic development has been reached, medical advances and health care do little to explain the improvements in the health of populations in the long run. Inequality in health among their populations has been one of the most prominent concepts in health policy in the UK, Norway, Finland, Sweden, Germany and other European countries, both East and West, ever since the 1970s, dating particularly from the publication of the Black Report in the UK in 1980 (see Department of Health and Social Services 1980). In these countries the field of inequality in health has been almost entirely preoccupied with understanding why

Table 5.2 Life expectancy in Bethnal Green, 1842

No. of deaths		Average age of the deceased
101	Gentlemen and persons engaged in professions, and their families	45 years
273	Tradesmen and their families	26 years
1258	Mechanics, servants, and labourers, and their families	16 years

differences in health by socio-economic status arise, persist, and even grow greater. This preoccupation is less evident in the United States, where a particularly varied population – ethnically and geographically – makes the idea of social class equality in health more complex.

In the UK there has been a tradition of a public health concern about 'unequal' health ever since the mid-nineteenth century, when Chadwick described the living conditions of the poor and showed that defective drainage, unsafe water and overcrowding were inevitably associated with a low expectation of life. In areas such as Bethnal Green in London, for instance, 'labourers' and their families had life expectancies less than half those of 'gentlemen' (see table 5.2).

Amidst the industrial revolution, the pioneers of public health focused on the social and physical environment as a primary cause of disease. Concern about inequality within the population remained in the early years of the twentieth century, and was offered as one major justification for the setting up of the National Health Service in 1948, following upon the Beveridge Report of 1942. The 'rediscovery' of inequality was signalled by the setting up and the reporting of the Working Group on Inequalities in Health, the Black Report, in 1980. In the following decades many other nations took up the issue, and the World Health Organization (Europe) issued discussion papers on the concepts and principles of equity in health within nations (Whitehead 1990) and chose the theme as one of those around which its strategy was based (World Health Organization 1998).

The nature and extent of inequalities

We are concerned here with ideas rather than statistics, and the data on 'inequalities' is immense, particularly in the UK, the Nordic countries, and to a lesser extent the other countries of Europe. A few examples will simply show the kind of evidence which is being used and, in particular, the way in which inequality in health is being defined.

In Europe, it has been usual to rely on occupation-based measures of social class or 'socio-economic status' to demonstrate inequality. This type of classification has been used in the UK for almost a century to capture the gradient of status in society. The original scheme ranged from Social Class I, professional occupations, to Social Class V, unskilled manual occupations, and the categorization can be condensed into simple comparisons between 'non-manual occupations' (Social Classes I–IIIa) and 'manual occupations' (Social Classes IIIb–V). Increasingly, this scheme is seen to have problematic features in modern society, and other measures are used besides social class, or other scales devised. In the USA, it is most common to employ combined scales of education and income.

Using the standard classification, however, the following are some typical observations.

- In the UK, life expectancy at birth is around nine years longer in Social Class I than in Social Class V. While the comparison of different nations has many problems (of definitions of social class, or adequacy of data sets), all comparative studies across developed Western nations show the same gradient. Kunst et al. (1998), for instance, compared death rates by class in eleven European countries. The probability of dying between the ages of forty-five and sixty-five for men in manual classes, compared with non-manual classes, was about equally large (five to seven times) for Sweden, Norway, Denmark, England and Wales, Ireland, Italy, Spain and Portugal. Finland and France had the most unfavourable ratios, of 9.8 and 11.5 times respectively.

- Certain regions within countries show consistent health disadvantages over others. Within each region there may be pockets of greater deprivation associated with higher mortality, but for any given level of deprivation the experience of different regions still varies.

- The experience of ill health also varies by social class, though not always as strongly or as regularly as death rates: in one national UK survey, 64 per cent of people over forty years old in manual classes defined their own health as only 'fair' or 'poor', compared with 52 per cent of those in non-manual classes (Cox et al. 1993).

- Class systems, or other socio-economic categories, are not the only dimensions of inequality: everywhere, minority or migrant ethnic groups tend to have higher death rates than the majority population.

- There are strong and universal differences between men and women: in all countries where there are no longer overwhelming dangers attached to childbirth, women live longer than men. However, they also tend to suffer more illnesses. To what extent these can be called 'inequalities' is a matter for debate.

Two aspects of the statistics on inequality have attracted particular attention of recent decades. One is that, measured by social class and by death rates, inequality appears to be increasing. In the UK, life expectancy in men in Social Class I increased from 72 to 77.8 years between the early 1970s and the mid-1990s. For men in Social Class V it increased from 66.5 to 68.2 years. There was, therefore, a gap which over twenty years had grown from 5.5 to 9.5 years. (For women, the increase in the gap was somewhat less.) Simply comparing Class I with Class V may be misleading, since each contains only small and changing proportions of the population. However, combining Classes I/II and IV/V to give greater numbers, around 1980 death rates of men were 53 per cent higher in Class IV/V than in I/II, but around 1990 they were 68 per cent higher. These growing differentials were also apparent for many of the major individual causes of death. There is a need to explain how, in many other developed nations, in the virtual absence of absolute deprivation, similar inequalities can persist and even become greater.

The second issue relates to what is known as the 'continuous gradient' or 'fine grain' of inequality. In countries where large proportions of the people live in extreme deprivation, or among the poorest minorities which still exist even in developed countries, it is not surprising that health is poorer or life expectancy less. What requires explanation is the fact that the 'threshold model' does not seem to be correct, that is, that 'inequality' relates only to a level of deprivation below which health is likely to be affected, even in comparatively wealthy societies where most people are likely to be above this level. There is no sharp discontinuity between the minority who lack the basic needs of life, or are exposed to the worst environmental hazards, and the majority whose living conditions meet at least minimum standards. Rather, a straight relationship between socio-economic status and health is found everywhere: health is socially patterned from the bottom to the top of the social scale. This is not a new finding: it has been known ever since national figures of death rates by social class were first produced. Only more recently has it been recognized that it extends – though with perhaps less regularity – to the experience of illness as well as to death rates, that it can be demonstrated to exist throughout the grades of one occupation (the civil service) in the UK (Marmot and Feeney 1996), and that it is an international phenomenon.

One of the most important arguments from the 1970s concerned the possible identification of a *general* susceptibility to ill health related to social class inequalities. The regular pattern of mortality by social class suggests that influences other than polluted environments, dangerous work, smoking and poor diets, which might account for particular forms of ill health, must be involved. It can be suggested that part of the rationale behind the extensive work which identified factors such as stress, lack of control, Antonovsky's *saluto-genesis*, and other psychological explanations involved the search for general causes that might map onto these general patterns. While the effect of specific causes, such as smoking, known to be differentially distributed between social classes, is undoubted, the regular differences in health up and down social scales seemed to be related to generalized differences in susceptibility to disease (Marmot et al. 1984). This work was crucial in turning attention away from single 'unhealthy' behaviours, or a simple emphasis on particular material factors, to a wider concept of social relationships.

However, it has more recently been suggested that attention should return to the patterns of prevalence and death associated with particular diseases. Davey Smith et al. (2001), for instance, reviewing life-course approaches to class inequality, suggest that this paradigm, linking stress to general susceptibility, may conceal the true complexity of the issue. Overall statistics of inequality in death rates are strongly influenced by a few important causes of death – CHD, stroke, lung cancer and respiratory disease – which show large socio-economic differences. During the last century, these diseases became the most important and their social gradient became steeper. But different conditions are influenced in different ways – some specially by early-life causes, and some by behaviours or environments in adulthood. These are diseases which usually show themselves only after relatively long exposure to risk factors, and the social gradients are due to the social circumstances within which lives are played out. Looking at specific diseases can contribute to more complex and satisfactory models of what we mean by social class inequality in health.

The causes of inequality

The main issue of debate is the *cause* of inequality in health, especially the causes of the apparent increase in inequality in the Western world. What are the precise mechanisms by which social inequalities affect health and how do patterns of health inequality develop over the life-course? What are the mechanisms by which health of populations is related to structural features of societies? The answer to these questions are at the same time essential for policy-makers who wish to reduce inequalities, and part of the story about how health is defined in contemporary Western society.

The Black Report in the UK (1980) discussed three types of explanation of 'real' inequalities, if the demonstrated social class differences were not simply artefacts of statistics and the changing composition of social classes over time. It was shown that in fact, although there were indeed problems of measurement, they did not change the broad picture or make inequality 'disappear'. The three remaining types of explanation were explanations of natural and social selection involving health-related mobility; explanations relating to the lifestyles and health-related habits of different groups in society; and materialist or structural explanations which focus on the direct effects of living and working conditions. Macintyre (1997) pointed out that for each of these there is a 'hard' and a 'soft' version. The 'hard' version is that a favoured type of explanation is the only cause of (or explains away) social variation in health. The 'soft' version, on the other hand, recognizes that the types of explanation are not exclusive, and each makes a contribution. She noted that the Black Report, while seeing material factors as the most important, and rejecting the 'hard' versions of the other explanations, did not suggest that the 'soft' versions were untrue or irrelevant. Some of the debate of the 1980s which followed the Black Report took up unhelpfully polarized positions, concentrating attacks on the 'hard' versions of explanation: this seemed to be necessary in a political climate in the UK where it was felt important to stress the material causes of increasing inequality.

In the last decade or so a more productive, though inevitably more complicated and difficult, effort has been made to explore the interrelation between and contribution of different types of explanation. Life-course studies are showing that selection by health certainly takes place, with the healthy moving up the social scale and the unhealthy suffering occupational disadvantage, but this does not explain away inequality as no more than the inevitable consequence of this social sorting. The concept of health capital, introduced in chapter 3, is relevant. Cohort studies which follow populations from the day of their birth demonstrate its utility. Wadsworth (1991), for instance, has shown, in relation to a British cohort born in 1946, how health capital accumulates or is dispersed. A poor start in life, associated with poorer parental socio-economic circumstances and vulnerability to illness, can be reinforced throughout childhood by poorer education and thus lower social class in adulthood, less healthy behaviour, and poorer health. The 'imprint of time' takes place over the individual life-course but also depends on historical time: if the social environment changes, each cohort has a unique health history.

Simple models which stress only the importance of behavioural patterns and voluntarily chosen lifestyles (with health education as the obvious remedy) have to allow for the facts that lifestyles depend on social relationships and histories and the cultures of areas and groups. Bourdieu's key concept of *habitus*, explaining how routine practices are influenced by the external structure of individuals' social worlds and in turn reproduce this structure (already discussed in chapter 4), is also relevant. The materialist explanations have been given weight by the wealth of evidence that inequality in health is directly associated with income, occupational status and disadvantaged areas. Even here, however, 'hard' versions have to be tempered by consideration of relative, rather than absolute, poverty, and the consideration of psychosocial mechanisms as well as direct physical effects.

The socio-biologic translation

The phenomenon of increasing inequality, and the pattern of a regular gradient up and down the social scale, requires explanations in biological terms. Dysfunction, disease and death must have actual physiological causes. Throughout life, it is easy to see how the most obvious insults – pollution, diet, hygiene, accidents, harmful work, poor housing – harm health, but it is difficult to see them as more than a partial explanation for gradients throughout the social scale.

It is agreed that the mechanisms are not, largely, genetic. For instance, it has been estimated that straightforward genetic inheritance may account for between only 1 and 5 per cent of the total disease burden, and indirect evidence such as blood grouping shows that social classes are genetically mixed, not homogeneous. Events associated typically with mothers in poor circumstances which occur at or before birth are certainly demonstrated to cast life-long shadows in terms of poor or 'unequal' health, but again they are only a partial explanation. Inequality in health grows greater as individuals grow older.

Thus a need is felt for what Tarlov (1996: 71) called the socio-biologic translation: the way in which social characteristics are perceived, processed into biological signals, and converted into actual disease. It has long been known that distress, grief and other damaging emotions can harm physical health: this is part of the social model. That psychological stress can also contribute to mental illness, or effect health-damaging behaviour, is obvious, but the search has been for specific biological mechanisms by which it can be transformed into specific diseases or into general susceptibility. The biological systems known to be concerned are common to most mammals: on perceiving threat or danger, the body is prepared for flight or fight through the endocrine and nervous systems, and adverse consequences for health result if arousal is sustained or constantly recurring.

The concepts which are invoked to provide the link to social circumstances are those such as feelings of control, self-efficacy and social cohesion. Low social status engenders psychological distress which is expressed in feelings such as shame, lack of self-esteem, and lack of dignity and respect. It is known within psychology that insecurity and the disturbed family functioning that may arise in adverse social situations in early childhood makes people more vulnerable in adulthood. Children brought up with different experiences of attachment and conflict use different strategies to cope with the stresses of threatening environments. Stressors, particularly those which are long-term, are unevenly distributed in society, to a large extent parallel, and cumulative, with material resources. Practical coping and buffering resources – education, access to help, useful networks – which might help to alleviate the effects of stress are similarly differentially distributed by social class. Thus biological science, psychology and sociology come together to flesh out the possible mechanisms of the socio-biologic translation.

This area of research and discussion about health inequality at the level of individuals within any given society is raised to the level of explaining the health of societies by the work of Richard Wilkinson and others. Wilkinson (1996) noted that, even though the health differences within societies are closely related to socio-economic status, once a country has reached a certain state of economic development, the population can be, as a whole, more than twice as rich as another country without being healthier:

> Despite the strong relationships between income and health that have been found repeatedly within countries, when you look at differences *between* the rich developed countries, you find – at best – only a weak relationship between their average incomes and their standards of health. For instance, even after allowing for price differences, Greeks have less than half the average income of Americans and yet are healthier. Similarly, although life expectancy in most developed countries tends to increase by two or three years every decade, this improvement it not closely related to economic growth: one country's economy can grow twice as fast as another's for perhaps twenty years and yet its citizens may not benefit from any additional growth in life expectancy. Income differences appear to be important within rich countries, but not between them. Even among the fifty states of the USA, where cultural differences are smaller than those between countries, there is (after allowing for differences in income distribution) no relationship between mortality and average state income. Yet within each state there is a clear link between income and health. (Wilkinson 2000: 10)

Wilkinson suggested that the most plausible explanation was that what matters to health, after a certain stage of development has been reached, is *relative* income and social status, not absolute income. The extent of social inequalities within nations is both a cause and an indicator of the health differences between nations. This relates not only to income inequality, but also to inequality in power and status. The greater the inequality in a society, manifested by authoritative power patterns and undemocratic institutions, as well as by a particularly unequal distribution of income and wealth, the poorer the health of that society. Material inequality engenders social divisions, which result in anxiety, conflict and other negative emotions, from which health status suffers. The mechanisms of the association can also be indirect, through behaviours ranging from alcohol and tobacco use to violent crime or the prevalence of firearm use. Countries with less social inequality, in contrast, tend to have more security, social support, trust and self-respect, all conducive to better health.

This thesis is supported by many studies which show that more equal countries, with smaller income differences between rich and poor, tend to have better health statistics, as measured not only by surveys of self-assessed health but also by mortality rates. Among the developed countries, it is the most egalitarian, not necessarily the richest, which have the highest life expectancy. Wilkinson suggests, for instance, that Japan, which by the end of the 1980s had become the country with the highest life expectancy in the world, seemed a highly cohesive society, with a long period of narrowing income differences and, uniquely in the developed world, falling crime rates. The relationship between income inequality and death rates has been shown both at the level of regions within countries and as comparisons between countries. As Wilkinson noted, this applies, for instance, in the fifty states of the USA, independently of average incomes, or the proportion of the population in absolute poverty, or expenditure on medical care.

Neo-materialist explanations

Other commentators have put forward a slightly different explanation for the relationship between health and income distribution within societies, criticizing too great an emphasis on psychosocial processes, and considering a broader set of social determinants of health. For instance, Coburn (2000) suggests that the psychosocial effects of perceived relative deprivation are less important than the fact that in more equal societies a wide range of factors, including public services, are more likely to be available to the whole population. The more market-oriented or neo-liberal the regime, the greater the inequalities and the more the social fragmentation. Economic globalization and competition associated with the international spread of neo-liberalism increase income, but they are also a cause of greater economic inequality, poorer cohesion, and more inequality in health. The effect of inequality may depend on the availability of public services. In unequal societies, such things as housing, health care or education may present problems for those who are relatively poor. Countries which have stronger forms of welfare do not exclude those with low incomes from their health benefits and tend to demonstrate better overall health than those most characterized by neo-liberal doctrines. This is suggested as a more important difference than the perception of social hierarchies.

Social capital

These types of explanation, to the extent that they emphasize the concept of social cohesion, are to some extent a return to Durkheim, and the demonstration that 'social facts' are more than the sum of individuals and that social health is related to social norms, social solidarity and the collective consciousness. The relevant concept of 'social capital' has, for several decades, driven one of the most active fields of discussion and research about the relationship of society and health. It is proposed as a way of explaining how community-level influences impinge on health, and embraces all the social, economic and cultural resources to which a population or group has access.

Essentially, it can be a version of communitarianism: social capital originates in community networks and voluntary organizations, because these settings provide potential for cooperative action and social support. Social connectedness or cohesion is generated by networks: this is what holds communities together and enables them to act for the common benefit.

The best-known proponent is the political scientist Robert Putnam, who credited Coleman with first having developed the theoretical framework. Coleman (1988) had defined the concept as

> not a single entity but a variety of different entities, with two elements in common. They all consist of some aspect of social structures, and they facilitate certain actions of actors – whether persons or corporate actors – within the structure. Like other forms of capital, social capital is productive,

making possible the achievement of various ends that in its absence would not be possible.

It was essentially a property of *communities*, not individuals. As Coleman went on to say, 'It is not lodged either in the actors themselves or in physical implements of production.'

Putnam (1995: 67) used it to explain the findings from a twenty-year study of regional government in Italy. He suggested that,

> For a variety of reasons, life is easier in communities blessed with a substantial stock of social capital. In the first place, networks of civic engagement foster sturdy norms of generalized reciprocity and encourage the emergence of social trust. Such networks facilitate coordination and communication, amplify reputations, and thus allow dilemmas of collective action to be resolved . . . At the same time, networks of civic engagement embody past success at collaboration, which can serve as a cultural template for future collaboration. Finally, dense networks of interaction probably broaden the participants' sense of self, developing 'I' into the 'we', or . . . enhancing the participants' 'taste' for collective benefits.

In research, various approaches and definitions of the concept have been used. Four may be distinguished:

- *Coleman's* definition of social capital as the structures of relationships in society, involving norms, obligations, relationships, sanctions, and access to resources
- *Putnam's* description as features of social organization such as norms, networks and social trust that facilitate coordination and cooperation for mutual benefit
- *Bourdieu's* more specific definition: the aggregate of resources, linked to membership of groups, which provide collectively owned capital
- *Portez's* application of the idea more clearly to individuals, defining social capital as the ability of actors to secure benefits by virtue of membership in social networks or other social structures.

The definition most commonly used is that of Putnam, and the key constructs within the concept are social relationships and networks, group affiliation and civic activity. Trust, developed through norms of reciprocity or mutual help, and networks of engagement in public affairs, are crucial. The research which attempts to test the concept tries to measure such things as social support, reciprocity, neighbourliness and feelings of belonging, activity in local groups (including religious groups), trust both in the people around and in local institutions, self-perceived control, power and influence over decisions, and feelings of exclusion or inclusion in the community. These are the things which come to define community 'health'.

They are necessarily usually 'measured' at the individual level by asking questions of people, and the answers aggregated to represent the community, but societal-level characteristics can also be used to represent what has been called the embeddedness or autonomy of groups. Statistics such as overall voting levels can be used as a measure of civic participation. There are also attempts to find indicators which can in some sense stand in for social cohesion, trust and reciprocity. For instance, it has been found that crime statistics, in the United States, and even such a simple measure as levels of gun ownership (which is of course correlated with crime and violence), are associated at geographical levels with income inequality (with average *level* of income taken into account). It is suggested that what is being identified is normative structures which encourage or inhibit crime, and this says something about social cohesion. The attempts to explain patterns of health change in Russia and other countries of the former Eastern bloc are also relevant (Bobak et al. 2000)

Some critical views have been raised about these models (Foley and Edwards 1999). It has been suggested that, in the studies finding associations between income inequality and population mortality, there are conceptual difficulties in using aggregate cross-sectional data as a means of testing hypotheses about the effect of income and its distribution on the health of individuals. Any focus on current incomes may in any case be too crude an indicator of accumulated health influences over life-times. Social capital theory has been criticized because of some ambiguity about the meaning and definition in practice of 'community', because the actual measures of 'commitment' or 'engagement' are held to be too oriented to middle-class values, and because close networks can be oppressive rather than supportive, or – in the example of, for instance, drug-using communities – health-harming rather than health-enhancing. Kunitz (2001: 170) notes that the quest for community ('certainly in the US, perhaps the most individualistic of nations') does not invariably lead to improved health, 'for social ties may bind us together, but they may also imprison us.'

Social capital is an attractive model, bringing together the tradition of research on 'stress' in the social model of health and the socio-biologic translation, with explanations for population health, in ways appealing to policy-makers. Muntaner et al. (2000: 107) described social capital as

> an alternative to the structural inequalities of class, gender, race, by bringing to the forefront of social epidemiology an appealing common-sense social philosophy to which everyone can relate, that is, good relations with your community are good for your health.

But it is argued that the concept neglects the distributive dimension, the way in which different societies distribute power and resources, economically and politically. The concept gives great importance to voluntary organizations and community groups, but the extent to which these have any influence or potential to contribute must depend on particular systems of checks and balances, ways of administration – in other words, their relationship, in a given country, to the state. Different linkages have different degrees of significance, and may – especially those likely to make up the networks of the less privileged – have no power at all, or, like the trades unions, have less than they did.

Kunitz (2001) points to the roots of the idea of social capital in the nineteenth century, originally in the work of Durkheim and de Tocqueville, who were responding to the political pressures of their own time: 'but our world is different from theirs.' At the level of individual health, he illustrates

> some of the ways in which the larger context may influence the structure, functions, and effectiveness of social networks, and how they may in turn influence various dimensions of people's health and use of services. That is to say, social rela-

tions are not always supportive and may be damaging. This is particularly so when poverty, unemployment, insecurity and inadequate infrastructure of formal organisation are prevalent. (Kunitz 2001: 167)

Considering particularly the application of the concept in the USA, he points to the legacy of civic cultures implanted in the North and the South as relevant to the higher social capital and lower mortality in the North. For the inequalities of metropolitan areas and the industrial heartland, the social history of the late nineteenth and early twentieth centuries must be invoked. The history and structure of specific populations and places are related both to social networks and to health. Qualitative work on social capital in the UK has also shown clearly (Swann and Morgan 2002) that the networks, social engagement, trust, reciprocity and cohesion which make up the currency of social capital research have to be linked with local cultures, social histories and policy environments. Since socio-political settings are so relevant, social capital must take different forms in different countries, and cannot be expected to be the same everywhere.

Discussion continues, but these ways of looking at health remain perhaps the most interesting contemporary ideas about health and society. In particular, they draw attention to the importance of considering health in positive terms – asking what affects the body's defences – rather than simply in negative terms as exposure to external material hazards. They lead, finally, to some consideration of the postmodern view of health, and where ideas about health are currently moving.

6
Where is the Concept of Health Going in the Contemporary World?

We live, of course, in a time of explosive change and development in medical science and technology. New knowledge and new techniques offer longer life and more control over our bodies, at least in those societies wealthy enough to afford them. At the same time there are new failures – the resurgence of tuberculosis, the appearance of antibiotic-resistant bacteria, the long struggle to control HIV/AIDS, unexpected diseases such as New Variant CJD or the new respiratory virus spreading world-wide in 2003 – and some perception among the public that 'modern living' creates its own illnesses, so that the sick person wonders:

> Are we dealing with an illness of the individual or with an illness of society? Is cancer part of myself, or does it come to me from the outside world? (Herzlich and Pierret 1987: 65)

The theme of this chapter is not the overambitious one of predicting where the art and science of medicine may be going, but rather to examine these contemporary trends in order to speculate on whether they are causing changes in fundamental definitions of health and illness. It will be suggested that there are changing boundaries between ill and not-ill, changing boundaries between life and death, and changing boundaries between self and not-self. Also, technological change in the delivery of medicine may produce new definitions of the patient.

Changing boundaries between ill and not-ill

The 'surveillance society' described in chapter 5 rests on technological developments. It requires not only ever more sophisticated measures and instruments, but also an administrative apparatus that can survey and screen populations. Essentially, it is creating boundaries for 'normality'. Any sharp divisions between healthy and not-healthy are replaced by a continuum: there is 'normal' variation, and even to be outside it is not necessarily 'ill', but may be *potentially* ill. Medicine targets everyone, not just those diagnosed as diseased, and everyone is to some degree at risk: as Armstrong (1995: 400) notes, it is

> a world in which everything is normal and at the same time precariously abnormal, and in which a future that can be transformed remains a constant possibility.

The 'remission society' described by Frank (chapter 1) is also relevant. People are not only potentially ill, but ill-in-remission, or ill but technologically returned to (functional) 'normality' by prostheses, pacemakers, transplants, and mechanical body regulators of many kinds. The triumph of modern medicine is that so many people have their lives prolonged by these means. The problem is that people are left 'needing a new map for their lives' (Frank 1995: 10).

As knowledge about disease and its measurable, though not necessarily experienced, precursors increases, and tests – blood tests, amniocentesis, genetic screening – become possible, new diseases-in-waiting are created. Techniques of diagnosis – mammography, screening for prostate cancer – make it possible to identify potential problems. They also, however, can give rise to anxieties, since the tests may be indeterminate or give results only in terms of relative risks. The knowledge of these may offer difficult choices, such as prophylactic surgical removal of the breasts or prostate. It is difficult to make rational decisions about these, since the risks are rarely precise. Acting and not acting both have costs. Thus there are debates about breast cancer screening – undoubtedly life-saving for some, but traumatic (because of false negative and false positive results) for many. People who are HIV-positive are, again, an example of the potentially but not yet ill. Thus, the discussion of HIV testing in the 1980s – before better therapies for prolonging life with HIV became available, so that tests had definite advantages for the individual – raised in stark form the disadvantages, both social and psychological, of choosing to enter the disease-in-waiting state, and the tension between these and the necessity to promote testing for public health purposes.

Mechanic (2002) suggested that screening and prevention are not only technologically driven but shaped by contemporary values – market competition, faith in modern technical progress, activism and consumerism. They may 'take patients on treatment trajectories that are difficult to control and which result in being labelled with diagnoses they do not have and receiving interventions they do not need' (p. 459). The 'gift of knowing' (Kenen 1996: 1547) is a questionable gift:

> Technology is Circe – handmaiden of the medical profession. The media, some health care professionals and informal kinship and friendship networks bombard individuals (mainly those with comprehensive health insurance) with messages about the value of recent biotechnical breakthroughs.

In cultures which promote activism and self-responsibility, there are difficulties about doing nothing if one is told one has or may have cancer, and individuals are pressured both socially and psychologically to consider aggressive treatment. These are extreme cases, but the same applies to less dramatic conditions and more routine tests, performed out of administrative habit (or sometimes out of commercial pressures), or simply because they are possible.

In a medical model, 'at risk' and 'abnormal' become confused. Similarly, in lay discourse, 'proneness' to illness consists of a mixture of ideas about heredity, immune status, individual make-up, and the consequences of health history:

'She's not one to take colds'; 'All the family are prone to arthritis'; 'I've been liable to depression ever since that event'; 'I'm healthy but prone to migraine.'

This confusion is especially fostered by the 'new genetics', that is, the body of knowledge and practice based on recombinant DNA technology, exemplified by the Human Genome Project, the great international enterprise which was directed towards mapping out the whole of the human genetic structure. This technology may present many future problems associated with the possibility of predicting health risks based on genetic make-up. How will these be used in the contexts of employment and insurance? Genetic screening is already common (at least in the USA) in industries such as chemicals, electronics, oil and pharmaceuticals, to identify those who may be 'genetically susceptible'. Again, there are opposing movements: that towards social responsibility, and that towards individuals' rights to privacy and ownership of the information contained in their own body.

Meanwhile, genetic testing for disease involves two groups of conditions. In late-onset dominant conditions, the inheritance of a single copy of a gene puts the individual at risk of developing disease. Genetic markers for Huntingdon's Disease, for instance, have been available since the mid-1980s. Hereditary breast and ovarian cancer are other conditions for which testing programmes are available, and predictive testing at any time throughout life can offer the likelihood of developing the disease. On the other hand, there are recessive conditions where individuals who inherit a faulty gene from both parents will inevitably develop the condition (examples include cystic fibrosis or Tay–Sachs Disease) at birth or early in life. Those who inherit a single copy will be carriers, who will not have the disease themselves but will pass it on to, on average, half their offspring.

Each of these presents difficult, but different, problems associated with the definition of health. The foetus may be tested, raising the possibility of avoiding the birth of potentially unhealthy children through abortion. In some cultures and from some ethical positions the 'selection' of healthy babies in this way is unacceptable. Predictive testing for late-onset conditions provides the opportunity to 'know' one's fate, but there are psychological and emotional difficulties in receiving this information if therapy is not available. Those diagnosed as having an increased possibility – or even the certainty – of developing disease may spend a lifetime as what Kenen (1994) called PPDs (Possible Potentially Diseased) or DIWs (Diseased in Waiting) with all the probable distress or discrimination that this entails. These issues are stark in a single gene disorder such as Huntingdon's, where disease is, at present, inevitable in an individual who lives long enough. On the other hand, unless those at risk of late-onset disease, or carrying recessive conditions, are tested, they may pass disease on to their children unknowingly. There are added complications if only some forms of a disease are related to a specific gene: it is thought, for instance, that this applies to only 3 to 5 per cent of cases of ovarian cancer.

When a disease is defined as genetic it moves from being an individual issue to being a family disease. Genetic risk becomes even more clearly a moral issue: in a study in the UK of women attending genetic counselling for heredity breast/ovarian cancer, they

> perceive themselves as having a responsibility to their kin (past, present and future generations) to establish the magnitude of their risk and the risk to other family members, and to act on this information by engaging in some form of risk management'. (Hallowell 1999: 597)

To pass on a gene, Hallowell notes, is not 'fault', but it is certainly 'a kind of responsibility'. Many studies have demonstrated the way in which families construct the meaning of hereditary risk within their everyday lives and how in turn these constructions shape the experience of predictive testing. Michie et al. (1996), for instance, described the role of 'functional pessimism' and 'uncertain wellness' in the case of the familial disease adenomatous polyposis. Cox and McKellin (1999) discussed how, in the case of Huntingdon's Disease, families adapted and modified their understanding of scientific risk, jointly engaging in a fluid and contingent 'social calculus of risk'.

Where prophylactic measures are available, as for breast and ovarian cancer, screening may be made available and used by those who believe, from their family history, that they are susceptible or 'prone' to the disease. Research has shown how prophylactic surgery can be seen by patients as both securing and undermining their present and future self-identities. Failure to take advantage of screening, not 'wanting to know', can be seen as morally irresponsible. However, if screening suggests action then this produces competing risks. In the case of ovarian cancer, Hallowell and Lawton (2002) described women's dilemmas in terms of maintaining or losing fertility, and maintaining or losing femininity, rather than ideas of 'illness', with the women saying, for instance: 'That's part of you being taken away, really, that's part of your role on earth being removed' (p. 434); 'ageing before your time', or 'for potential risk when I'm 80, I've wrecked my life now' (p. 437).

It is commonly suggested that the new genetics not only creates these ill/not-ill dilemmas for the individual, but is affecting the whole discourse of health and illness. The gene is becoming an icon, perhaps especially in American society, and a kind of genetic fatalism – assuming that genetic make-up determines a wide range of behaviour and 'innate' characteristics – underlies much public discourse. Conrad (1999) notes that genetic explanations are readily accepted by the public, even in cases where the evidence is limited, and there is a sense in which popular views of genetics look backwards in terms of concepts of health. The model is of specific etiology, where one gene or genetic mutation can cause a disease or behaviour – the 'breast cancer gene', the 'obesity gene' – in what is called the OGOD (one gene, one disease) concept, with complex interactions and contextual effects ignored. Conrad suggests this shows parallels with the acceptance of germ theory in the early twentieth century, and is accepted because it resonates with it. At the same time it appeals to current Western ideas of individualism and self-responsibility, 'a naive form of genetic determinism that assumes (in language at least) that there are specific genes for specific traits under all circumstances.' In fact:

> Virtually everyone has some genes that make them suscepti-
> ble to diseases or traits we might find problematic. All of us

are genetically liable to some human trouble, be it allergies, nearsightedness, baldness, depression, or forms of heart disease or cancer. The trick is to understand how these susceptibilities interact with particular environments to produce or not produce human traits or disorders. (Conrad 1999: 238)

At the same time, the 'geneticization' of society can imply that health becomes de-individualized. Health becomes a family issue: to assess an individual's risk may involve their kin, and people become involved in complex networks of health (Wertz 1992). Genetic 'risk' becomes identified not in the specific body but in computer programmes of 'pedigrees' or family histories.

There are obvious concerns about where the new genetics may be taking medicine. The increasing use of DNA databases threatens what Nelkin and Andrews (1999) call 'surveillance creep', a controlling tool for organizations and governments. The role of corporate industry also becomes increasingly important, not only in shaping the therapy of gene technology but also in choosing the direction of research. A new speciality, pharmacogenetics, or the study of the genetic variation underlying the different responses that patients may have to drugs, has expanded rapidly with the completion of the Human Genome Project and the development of technologies which enable cheap genetic testing. Obviously, there are pressures on the pharmaceutical industry to identify the best drug doses and the patients who are going to be more or less responsive, possibly reducing adverse reactions, and there are pressures on health providers to supply drugs efficiently and reduce costs. The possibility is raised of routine genetic testing before prescribing.

Genetic screening produces not only new states in between health and illness for the individual, but also these wider new ways of thinking about disease and disability. Various types of genetic choice, from sex selection to personality traits, theoretically become available through new reproductive technologies, cloning, or gene therapy. Disability activists worry that genetic interventions will inevitably lead to a new form of eugenics, with a diminished value placed on people with disabilities. Now that the idea of genetic disease is no longer restricted to single-gene inherited disease but has been extended to many conditions such as heart disease, the possibility of gene therapy for a broad range of common acquired conditions tends to reconceptualize all illness within the language of molecular genetics.

Meanwhile, new technologies – including also the fields of organ transplantation and intensive care – are already raising ethical questions about the distribution of health resources. The issues raise concerns not only about who is ill, and what is disease, but also about who will be – inevitably – selected for 'treatment' and who will not.

Changing boundaries of life and death

It is not only the boundary between health and illness which is blurring, but the most fundamental boundary of all – that distinguishing life from not-life. This is particularly true at the beginning and the end of life.

At the beginning, developments in reproductive technology call into question when a new life commences. The identification of the precise moment is probably not something that can be assessed scientifically. Is it at fertilization? At implantation? At a certain stage of foetal development? Not until living apart from the mother? Decisions have to be made, however, especially in the context of contraception and abortion. Technologies associated with reproductive genetics present choices which are associated with the actual creation of life, with profound social consequences.

Technologies such as IVF and surrogate motherhood raise questions not only about fertility, but also about the definition of the family, and about the meaning of motherhood and fatherhood. Administrative and legal definitions have to be made about who, in what circumstances, is a mother, about the difference between a biological and a social father, and about who, under what circumstances, has what rights and obligations. New social roles are created, such as sperm donor or surrogate mother. Manipulation of eggs, sperm and embryos outside the body offers moral dilemmas: prenatal diagnosis or gene therapy for serious disease is generally acceptable, but 'designer babies' are not. Similarly, help for infertility is to be welcomed, but the turning of babies into commodities condemned.

Modern technological medicine has been accused of taking over both birth and death, and transferring them from the category of a normal part of 'healthy' lives to the medicalized realm of the pathological. It has been argued that the advent of hospital medicine was largely responsible for the handing over of birth and death to specialists and their removal from the public view. Death, in particular, became hidden, avoided, verging on the obscene. Commentators such as Aries noted how modern Western societies tended to deny death, seeing it as the enemy, often 'untimely', and a failure of medicine – almost an 'unnatural' event. The 'good' death, peaceful and accepting, is presented as an ideal, but an ideal that few are permitted to experience. At the same time, the wish for individual control which is held to be characteristic of late modern societies is now responsible for a desire to control one's own dying, as one's own childbearing, rather than hand it over to the system of medicine. Thus there is some shift (in Anglophone countries, though not necessarily in other cultures) to hospice and palliative care for the dying, and rising support for the right to make decisions about the manner and timing of one's own death (Seale 2000).

As with the precise definition of birth, however, the enlargement of scientific and therapeutic knowledge and the advance of technology raise questions about the definition of death. Does it occur when the brain is destroyed, or later, when the heart stops beating? It is questionable, in fact, whether (like the beginning of life) the end of life can ever be reduced to one point in time: death is biologically a process rather than an event. But modern techniques of 'keeping alive' demand a definition. Are people in a 'persistent vegetative state' – irrevocably unconscious and without the capacity for cognitive functioning – actually persons? Whose is the decision whether they should be kept, artificially, in this state? Their own, by their previously recorded choice, or that of their relatives, or their doctors? These ethical issues, born of technological advance, raise questions about the difference between life and death.

They are rendered particularly important and uncertain because a definition of death is needed for the removal of organs for transplant surgery. Healthy and functioning organs are required, and if they are to be procured from the 'dead', a legal moment of death must be recognized.

> With the assistance of technology we can postpone the physical death of patients whose entire brains are traumatized beyond hope of recovery. If the patient is not to become an organ donor, then usually the process is prolonged only briefly, while brain death is confirmed. When a brain-dead patient is to become a organ donor, then biological dying is postponed for a much longer period, specifically so that the body may be commodified. Here resides a new, technologically manipulated death. (Lock 2002: 120)

It is notable that, as Lock discusses, *different* moments are identified in different Western nations. The concept of 'brain death' – that is, that death occurs at the moment when the brain becomes irreversibly damaged – is apparently acceptable in many cultures, since high proportions of populations say that they would not wish to be 'kept alive' in such circumstances. On the other hand, it is not universally acceptable, and when the actual moment of decision arrives for relatives at the bedside, they require to have absolute confidence in doctors' judgement and the technology which is defining death. Even greater problems are raised by the technique of 'non-heart-beating cadaver donors', where patients are transfused with cold fluids immediately after cardiopulmonary death, so that organs remain in good condition until they can be removed.

The problems of both birth and death are combined with the possibility of 'foetal rescue', the keeping of a brain-dead mother alive in order to deliver a foetus. Definitions of birth and death, and of 'the person', are also raised by the use of cells from foetuses or stillborn infants for genetic therapy, or the possibility of using anencephalic infants as organ donors.

Changing boundaries between self and not-self

Assisted reproductive technologies, organ donation, and replacement of body parts artificially are also examples of technological developments associated with transformations of the body. The healthy body becomes more widely defined to include supplementation – the mechanical supplementation of artificial joints, cardiac pacemakers and valves, ear implants, lenses for eyes, biochemical supplementation with drugs to cure imbalances, and physiological supplementation by the transplant of organs. A vast array of technologies becomes available to alter bodies – what Williams (1997) calls the 'transhuman bodyshop'. The body becomes increasingly 'bionic'. In 'cyber-medicine', with machine parts integrated into the body, human and machine become less and less distinct. In addition to these therapeutic developments, in an age of commercial 'healthism', body maintenance and plastic surgery, the healthy body also becomes plastic and can be reshaped and transformed. As Glasner (1995: 175) comments:

> If the period from the mid-1800s to the mid-1900s was one in which the individual's body became a vehicle for the display of consumer products, lately we are faced with the next logical step in consumerism. No longer can we merely dress up the body we happen to have, or improve it by losing weight or having a beauty makeover or straightening out the curve in our nose. We must actually purchase a 'new body'.

These contemporary medical practices, rather than challenging mind/body divisions, 'actually exacerbate them through a high-tech form of neo-Platonism' (Williams 1997: 1047). Organ transplants raise the mind/body dualism in a stark form: the heart becomes 'only a pump', a spare part, and not part of identity. Despite the many decades of discussion of the body as not a machine, of the way in which body and mind, or body and identity, cannot be separated, transplantation suggests that the body is not the same as the self. It is objectified: something which is possessed rather than something that one 'is'. Body parts may fail and need to be replaced; the body is a repairable machine. As Waldby (1998: 228) notes, medical technologies can never be understood as simply tools like other tools, because 'it is difficult to sustain a sense that "we" are the masters of medical technology when "we" are also its material objects.'

It is commonly noted that there is some feeling among those who become involved that, contrary to the machine metaphor, organs may transfer the donor's qualities to the recipient (Sanner 2001). This may be seen as a sort of magical thinking, beneath the surface of science (Sharp 1995), though it is also fostered by some practices in transplantation medicine:

> On the one hand, the language of medicine insists that human body parts are material entities, devoid of identity whether located in donors or recipients. However, in the rhetoric promoting donation, organs are animated with a life force, and donor families are not discouraged from thinking of their relatives as 'living on' in the bodies of recipients. Organ donation is very often understood as creating meaning out of senseless, accidental, horrifying death – a technological path to transcendence. All that donor families can hope for in the way of a return gift for this selfless act, however, is a letter of heartfelt thanks, often belated, written anonymously, and delivered through the local transplant coordination service with all identifying features deleted. . . . Reciprocity is reduced to an act of the imagination. (Lock 2002: 319)

Certainly some organs such as the heart are felt as more central to 'self' than others such as the kidney, and are harder to accept. There is evidence that organ recipients commonly experience identification with the donor, or a sometimes guilty sense that their health is at the expense of another life.

This suggests that there are still problems about the objectification of body parts. The giving of part of oneself can be represented as an altruistic choice, or even in some circumstances a duty, but it can also come uncomfortably close to the commercial arena. Certainly commodification of body parts – their buying and selling as commercial products – is anathema in the West (though it has to be noted that in many places blood is treated as a commodity). The possibility of exploitation of the poor, in the developing nations, raises recurrent scandals. Nevertheless the logic of transferable parts from one body to another, as of the transfer of sections of DNA from one individual to another, inevitably implies some return to reductionist models of the self. It also implies – indeed demands – new forms of public regulation.

Interchangeability crosses species in the case of xeno-transplantation, where transgenic animals (specially bred to carry genes from another species) are used as donors for organs. Studies show that the willingness to receive animal organs is considerably less than for receiving human organs, though other remedies of animal origin have long been accepted: incorporation of animal organs is seen as somehow challenging one's humanity. Animals may also be used for tissue engineering, though there is the promise of replacing the need for either human donors or those from other species by the actual fabrication of organs by using biodegradable plastics as substrates for cell culture, integrated into the body.

Stem cell technology is another development which is held to offer the promise of transformation of the way in which organs or tissue for transplantation are produced: 'from a social economy in which citizens donate whole organs to one in which embryos are a major source' (Waldby 2002). Stem cells – cells which can renew tissue in the body – might in future be induced to differentiate on demand, producing an unlimited supply of transplantable tissue. They could even provide alternative therapies for common disease. The use of embryos, for instance embryos 'left over' from IVF, for this purpose is seen by some as ethically problematic. Similarly, cloning techniques, and the birth of new siblings from selected embryos specifically so that cells might be retrieved from the umbilical cord to 'treat' the disease of existing children, are controversial. A single cell can, in theory, form the basis for therapeutic tissue for innumerable recipients over time. But what, Waldby asks:

> does it mean when the human body can be disaggregated into fragments that are derived from a particular person, but are no longer constitutive of human identity? . . . What is the status of such fragments, and how is the status of the individual (strictly speaking, the in-dividual, he who cannot be subdivided) altered to accommodate these possibilities for fragmentation? (Waldby 2002: 308)

The new technologies not only blur the distinction between body and not-body, but call into question human relationships and human identities. 'Health', as an attribute of an individual, may have to be rethought.

The information revolution and the definition of the patient

Other developments have the potential for changing the definition of the patient – and, indeed, the doctor. It has been suggested that the new technologies of medicine – from X-rays to computer tomography, magnetic resonance imaging, or CAT scans – privilege the 'image' over the actual body and its experiences. The image, not the body itself, forms the basis of medical practice. Drawing on the work of the French sociologist Baudrillard, Frank noted:

> Real diagnostic work takes place away from the patients; bedside is secondary to screen side. For diagnostic and even treatment purposes, the image of the screen becomes the 'true' patient, of which the bedridden body is an imperfect replica, less worthy of attention. In the screens' simulations our initial certainty of the real (the body) becomes lost in hyperreal images that are better than the real body. (Frank 1992: 83)

Baudrillard had argued that the movement into the high-tech postmodern world meant entrance into hyperreality. Imaging and visualization become central, the distinction between what is represented and its representation disappears, and simulations come to constitute 'reality'. In the wider society, the production of goods is replaced by the production of models and simulations, and the real and the image become difficult to distinguish. In medicine, screens and images externalize the interior of the body, which is converted into digital codes. Such techniques as microsurgery, keyhole surgery and nanotechnology (technology at the level of molecules) all place images between the doctor and the patient: indeed, machines replace the patient and, to a degree, the doctor.

Moreover, the use of telemedicine, or information technology used to support the delivery of health services, has been actively supported by health policy in Western medical systems for at least a decade. There are new kinds of links between clinicians and patients which mean that they need have no physical contact. This is attractive to policy, because it may offer solutions to some of the problems of access to care. It obviously has special application in places where population densities or special environments create problems for the supply of specialist services, such as Arctic areas, and parts of Australia, the United States and Canada. Medical telemetry (images and readings sent electronically), already part of space medicine, means that consultation (perhaps between several people) can take place at a distance. There can be 'automated' consultation, which means that personal contact need not be involved at all, or at least that patients can be screened before the involvement of a clinician. 'Virtual surgery' can be performed at a distance, and whole new disciplines such as teleradiology or teledentistry evolve.

Indeed, a whole new field of knowledge around the new information technologies in medicine has emerged, with new journals devoted to its knowledge base. At the level of the patient, new forms of communication provide a wider access to information: privileged access to knowledge is no longer the exclusive mark of the doctor, and the Internet loosens the boundaries between the lay person and the professional.

All this requires, however, a standardization of medicine. It implies agreement on evidence-based clinical facts and cannot be totally flexible. May et al. (2001) offer the example of the introduction of a relatively low-tech experimental videophone system, designed to facilitate the referral of patients with anxiety and depression in primary care to a community health team. They point out that there is not only 'hard technology' – the computer or videophone – but also 'soft technology' – the body of knowledge and the skills and interactional practices of doctors, and there can be conflict between the two. In this instance there were some reservations about the system on the part of doctors.

Moreover, the new imaging technologies tend to require very specialized knowledge, not universally shared. Prior et al. (2002) show how the new technologies and the new genetics come together when risks are 'assembled' in a cancer genetics clinic. Both computer programmes of family histories and techniques of producing images of DNA sequences require expert knowledge for their interpretation, and 'even though clinicians and laboratory professionals understand what goes on in the lab they understand it in different ways'

(p. 255). At each stage there is potential for seeing and assessing in different ways and from different standpoints. Making things 'visible' has to be of paramount importance.

As Wyatt (1996) notes, the new hard technologies favour specialities that use primarily on-screen data or images, or those where all the data can be seen as objective and measurable, rather than those that focus on the direct examination of patients in the context of their lives. Wyatt suggests that these developments are fundamentally 'technologically pulled' rather than 'clinically pushed' and inevitably produce pressures towards the standardization of disease symptoms and categories. All essentially 'laboratory' medicine, as May et al. (2001) noted, also breaks the immediate connection between consultation and diagnosis, which can be seen as attacking the whole culture of medical space and medical presence.

Health and illness in the postmodern world

For many theorists, this new era of computerized images and codes, this hyperreality, is the hallmark of what is called postmodernity, high modernity, or the late modern period. These are differently defined by various commentators, but in general postmodernity is held to be the condition which contemporary advanced industrialized societies are thought to have reached. The modernity which it replaces was defined as characterized by stability, security, the clear work patterns and stable hierarchies of manufacturing industry, and confidence in the advance of science (and thus confidence in medicine and doctors). Postmodernity is a period of segmented markets and a more complex and fragmented social structure. Industrial jobs are replaced by work in communications and services, work becomes more flexible, and job insecurity rises. Corporate capitalism and consumer lifestyles shaped by popular culture are dominant. The period is characterized by the rise of transnational companies and the expansion of the global economy. Change is become more common, social relations are in a state of flux, and life is more reflexive. Individuals are separated from their traditional ties and become linked, rather, by market relations. Identity is constructed around social practices and cultural consumption, and rather than being determined by the traditional categories of class, gender, age, race and so on becomes fluid and self-directed. In this context genetics individualizes, and genetic material becomes purely personal capital: as Prior (2000) says, it blocks out the problems of collectivities and 'highlights merely the particular, the singular, and the personal' (p. 199).

In a society characterized by change and adaptability, a sense of self is no longer 'given'. Elliott (2001: 136) described the three states of mind that define the core contours of postmodern selfhood:

> Firstly, there is an emphasis upon fragmentation. The postmodernist critique suggests that the contemporary self is so fragmented, multiple and dispersed that the symbolic consistency and narrative texture of experience disintegrates. In a world invaded by new technologies and saturated with flashy commodities, the self loses its consistency, and becomes brittle, broken or shattered. Secondly, the flickering media surfaces of postmodern culture are, according to this view, mirrored internally, so that a narcissistic preoccupation with appearance, image and style dominates the regulation of the self . . . Thirdly, there is a new centrality accorded to fantasy and phantasmagoria on the personal and social levels, so that the dream, hallucination and madness take on an added importance at the expense of common stocks of knowledge or rationality. In conditions of postmodernity, in the West at any rate, people seem to be experiencing a mixture of confusion, dispersal and disillusionment on the one hand, and excitement, desire and the possibility for personal development on the other.

How do concepts of health change in this postmodern world? Derrida's way of understanding its increasing complexity and heterogeneity has been influential: dualities and clear categories are deconstructed and shown as a particular way of 'knowing'. If health and illness are implied opposites, the dominant position, health, is created only out of the contrast with ill health.

The postmodern world is marked by what is spoken of as the 'end of tradition'. This includes a loss of faith in those traditionally seen as experts, including the medical profession. People are encouraged to make their own decisions – what the British sociologist Giddens calls the 'reflexivity of the self' – based on ever more numerous sources of information. Issues of health are increasingly attractive to the mass media, and bodies of information range from self-help manuals of all kinds to the changing, flexible, not always clearly legitimized World Wide Web. As Hardey (1999) has commented, the *users* of information, rather than the professional experts, begin to decide what is to be delivered to them. Traditionally, health education is directed and distributed by doctors and educators, but the Internet offers a view of health which is 'deprofessionized and demystified', making the provisional nature of medical knowledge more obvious.

There is a blurring of lay and medical knowledge. Debates about medical knowledge and medical ethics are made more public. At the same time that medicine becomes more 'scientific' and technological, a pluralistic view of health is encouraged, since information is supplied about different medical systems, and lay 'stories' begin to be included. There is greater openness towards complementary and alternative therapies, and increasing interest in them among a consumerist public, 'shopping' for care and cure.

All this reflects profound changes in medicine and in attitudes to health. The 'old' biomedical health care was characterized as curative, based in structures and institutions, and with the interaction between doctors and patients at its core. 'New' or postmodern medicine is preventive, not institutionalized, and multidisciplinary. Leisure is an industry, health promotion is individualized, and health itself is an international commodity. As Bunton and Burrows commented (1995: 207), 'health is idealised as self-governed lifestyle choice.' We live, as Wilkinson describes, in a 'cash and keys' society, constantly exposed to pressures from the market and constantly monitoring our own position in that market:

> Whenever we leave the confines of our own homes we face the world with the two perfect symbols of the nature of social relations on the street. Cash equips us to take part in transactions mediated by the market, while keys protect our private

gains from each other's envy and greed. What adds to the social potency of these arrangements is that instead of being marginal to our lives, they are the organising principles of the most highly interdependent system of production and consumption that has ever existed. Although we are all wholly dependent on one another for our livelihoods, this interdependence is turned from being a social process into a process by which we fend for ourselves in an attempt to wrest a living from an asocial environment. Instead of being people with whom we have social bonds and share common interests, others become rivals, competitors for jobs, for houses, space, seats on the bus, parking places. And yet, as social beings, we cannot treat others in the arena of public life simply as part of the natural environment: instead processes of social comparison – favourable or unfavourable – mean everything is constantly monitored. (Wilkinson 1996: 226)

The new flexibility and reflexive identity do not redress the old inequalities of health that were discussed in chapter 5. New stresses arise, transformed by socio-biologic processes into disease, and

although we may well be witnessing the emergence of late modern forms of self-identity it is not a uniform transformation across the population. Some actors have a much greater autonomy to construct their identities than others. Whilst some may be able to pay for cosmetic surgery others have to wait for unacceptably long periods just for routine relief from pain and other obstacles to their daily lives. Whilst some can afford to choose extra virgin olive oil and fresh vegetables, others have to sleep in cardboard boxes on the streets and eat what food they can get. (Bunton and Burrows 1995: 211)

The risk society

In this postmodern world, discourses of risk are pervasive. Since the appreciation of risk is the means by which individuals are encouraged to regulate their lives and bodies, this is associated with ideas of choice and responsibility. At the societal level, the imperatives which this new society requires are flexibility and a necessary amount of risk-taking.

In the 'modern', as opposed to the postmodern, world, risk was always one of the basic concepts of social epidemiology, in the form of risk factors for disease, relative risks of mortality, or predictors of particular types of ill health. Towards the end of the twentieth century, with a rising interest in the functional purposes of risk in an increasingly uncertain world, an industry developed concerned with risk and risk assessment. The 'rational' approach saw risk as a technical matter, to be tackled with more science and better information. From this point of view a basic premise is that all risks are measurable and possible to control. People's own perceptions of risk were not, it was recognized, necessarily in the same rational frame, and the psychology of risk or the relationship between lay and expert perceptions of risk became a prolific field of research. Anthropology pointed out that risks are culturally constructed, and variations in risk recognition and response are the products of different cultures, institutions and lifestyles (Douglas 1992).

Douglas had earlier formalized a schema (Douglas 1970) to analyse how people identified different risks in the context of their own form of social organization. This came to be known as grid/group analysis: 'grid' means 'the social distinctions and delegations of authority that they use to limit how people behave to one another', and 'group' is 'the outside boundary that people have erected between themselves and the outside world' (Douglas and Wildavsky 1982: 138). By combining grid and group, four distinct 'cultural biases' are identified in the context of risk, which were called hierarchist, egalitarian, fatalist and individualist. The implications of this were that people choose (not necessarily consciously) attitudes to risk and different types of behaviour which are most suitable for their own social organization and way of life.

In its specific application to health, this attention to the concept of risk is an essential part of the 'surveillance society'. Risk assessment became a key element of public health, and risk became the language of health education. Individualized 'risk factors' – smoking, overweight, a sedentary lifestyle – became almost synonymous with disease. The perception and management of voluntary risks, and the relative importance of these lifestyle factors and other environmentally and socially imposed health risks, were the central questions of health promotion and public health. As Prior (2000) notes, even the certainty of death is transformed into a private risk.

Death is no longer capricious and random, but simply a 'risk' which is in our own hands, with some sense of ultimate avoidability:

> Death, it seems, stalks only those that are careless of their own personal health. This, despite the fact that the mortality rates of those who are careless of their health and those who are fastidious remain stubbornly similar (viz 100 per cent). It is perhaps a frame of mind epitomised by the use among epidemiologists of the phrase 'avoidable death' – you too can avoid death if you have behaved yourself. (p. 193)

Expert and lay frames with regard to risk are, of course, bound to differ, and the concept of risk is inevitably full of paradox. The probabilities produced by risk analysis relate to groups, and can say nothing about the individual case. Given a relatively rare health event associated with common behaviours or characteristics, while most of those who experience it may have been 'at risk', most of those at risk will escape the event. In the case of risk status for coronary disease, for instance, Davison et al. (1991) demonstrated the prevalence of the idea of 'coronary candidacy', based on the wide range of conditions and behaviours that people had been taught, or had perceived through their own experience, as being causally linked to the onset of heart disease but recognized as not *necessary* causes:

> The candidacy system, then, has two interwoven strands. On the one hand is a set of criteria which can be used in the post-hoc explanation of illness and death, the prediction of illness and death, and the assessment of risk. On the other hand, there exists the all-important knowledge that the system is fallible. It cannot account for all coronary disease and death, neither can it account for the apparently unwarranted longevity of some of those that the system itself labels as candidates. Thus the observation that 'it never seems to happen to the people you expect it to happen to' becomes integrated as a central part of the system itself. (p. 15)

In part as a consequence of the limitations for epidemiology of the conventional individualized risk approach – it has been suggested, for instance, that when all known risk factors for coronary heart disease are considered together, they account for only about 40 per cent of the incidence of the disease – wider issues in postmodern society come to the fore. The concept of the 'risk society' (Beck 1992) has been particularly influential. Beck suggests that we live in a society which is increasingly interdependent, increasingly vulnerable to international catastrophe and to the risk management of organizations over which we have no control. Health risks – especially ecological, genetic, nuclear, but also the economic risks associated with global economies – are in the hands of 'experts' whose manner of assessment we may not even understand, and whom we may not trust. The erosion of trust is fostered by the growing recognition that these risks are often ultimately unknowable.

There is nothing new, of course, about the fact that life presents continual risks to the health of the individual. What is new is that the imposition of technological risks is recognized, publicized, feared and resisted by the population. Governments assume a duty to take preventive action, not usually by removing the risks but by suggesting ways of accommodating them. So potassium iodide is stored to be distributed to families within 2 kilometres of nuclear power stations against the possibility, however remote, of accident; in periods of perceived high risk of terrorist attack in public places the public are warned to be individually vigilant; travellers by air are recommended to use aspirin and compression stockings to guard against deep vein thrombosis. Simply to live in one's house, or journey to work, or travel abroad, is to expose oneself to harm-in-waiting. Not to take precautions against risks which may be quite remote is seen as dereliction of duty on the part of governments and carelessness on the part of the individuals.

At the same time the possibility of approaching health risks in their own lives rationally, and attempting to control them, is not evenly distributed in the population, so new forms of inequality, 'the inequality of dealing with insecurity and reflexivity', are created:

> The social positions and conflicts of a 'wealth-distributing society' become joined by those of a 'risk-distributing society'; social risk positions spring up, which are not exactly class

positions, but which are associated with them because the ability to deal with risk is unequally distributed in occupational and educational groups. (Beck 1992: 20)

Evolutionary medicine

The trends which have been considered – the postmodern changes in self and society, the rise of the risk society, and in particular the new genetics – lead, finally, to the most speculative developments in the contemporary definition of health, concerned with the 'new Darwinism' and what is called *evolutionary medicine*. These relate to quite fundamental changes in ideas about the public health and, indeed, the future of humankind.

An earlier, and not universally acceptable, version of this was the movement known as *sociobiology*. This applies to human behaviour, the Darwinian thesis that organisms must maximize their reproductive success. Genes that enable individuals to survive, within a particular environment, and have more offspring will increase over time as the result of natural selection. A basic tenet is that individuals, and hence their genes, are self-benefiting (described by the biologist Dawkins as the 'selfish gene'), and thus traits favourable for selection in the past will condition current behaviour. Individuals are genetically predisposed to certain behaviours because these maximized the fitness of their ancestors over previous generations. A corollary is that, when the environment changes, certain genes may become less well adapted.

In its crudest form, sociobiology was criticized as deterministic, and the Darwinian 'survival of the fittest' metaphor rejected as appearing to justify inequality or even racial discrimination. There were problems in talking of 'universal' human traits, in view of the diversity of human societies and behaviour. In particular, in classical Darwinian terms, it is heresy to ascribe intentionality or to assume that the existence of a characteristic is evidence that it must have evolved 'for a purpose': evolution is based on the occurrence of *random* variations between individuals, which either enhance or reduce chances of surviving (in a changing environment) to reproduce and pass genetic characteristics on to offspring.

More sophisticated forms of social Darwinism are exemplified by, for instance, Dickens (2000: 116), who suggests how 'evolutionary thought and social theory can be combined' by considering the way in which 'capital is modifying human biological structure in its own image'. Human biology evolves not by simple accident, but by manipulation – that is, by the exercise of social power. There is not only the possibility of deliberate genetic or other biological manipulation, but also a more subtle process – a 'gradual embedding' of a division between abstract and concrete thinking in the biological structure of the population. The power structure of modern society means that conceptual work is highly prized and rewarded, and practical work downgraded. Thus the social and the biological meet in selection according to certain types of aptitude and ability.

The movement known as *evolutionary ecology* distinguishes itself from social Darwinism, focusing on the interactions between the individual and the organism in specific environments. From this perspective, health is in part contingent on the difference between modern environments and those in which humankind evolved. It is observed that diseases have their own evolutionary history: the characteristics of diseases, as well as of individuals, are the products or by-products of adaptation by natural selection in a particular environment. Chisholm (1998) gives examples of the way in which various symptoms of 'pathology' are actually defence mechanisms, adaptive responses to a new environment. Fever in response to infection, women's reproductive cancers in modern industrial societies, pregnancy sickness, infant colic – all are pathologies which can be reinterpreted as adaptation to a changing environment:

> when people lack the resources to limit environmental risk and uncertainty they may be induced to grow and come to behave (most of the time probably quite unconsciously) in ways associated with earlier and/or frequent reproduction – *even at the cost* of decreased health, wellbeing and shortened lives. From an evolutionary perspective, this makes sense. Natural selection favours reproductive capacity, not health.
> (Chisholm 1998: 84)

As Chisholm points out, evolutionary theory can alter fundamentally the way we think about health and disease. There is tension between ends and means: having descendants, not health, is the 'goal' of life, and health is not always the best measure of adaptation. Questions are raised about the 'normal'.

There are important implications for both individual therapy and public health in understanding why particular diseases exist, and one may thus speak of *evolutionary medicine*. This is about 'exploring the implications for therapy of understanding the processes of adaptation that produce the evolutionary histories that culminate in a particular person, presenting with a particular complaint, at a particular place and time' (Chisholm 1998: 73–4). Fundamental questions are now raised about the basic concepts of agent, environment and host. The aim of public health becomes the reduction of environmental risk and uncertainty in order to achieve control over adaptation to change.

Western medicine, in the period which this volume has particularly considered, was founded in a very particular view of the world, that of the scientific biomedical model. At the beginning of the twenty-first century it seems, in Chisholm's words, 'poised to take the radical philosophical step of exploring how modern evolutionary theory might augment these venerable ways of knowing' (1998: 72). Many of the changes which have been discussed – new technologies and developments in the organization of medicine, new ways of seeing the body, postmodern fragmentation and flux, and confusion of the self and not-self, body and not-body – are altering the way in which health is perceived. The old certainties of single causes, generic diseases, the definition of ill health as deviation from the normal – even the doctrine of scientific neutrality – are all seen as problematic, and the pace of change leaves many contradictions and dilemmas.

There are, as always, tensions between the individual and the public health. The new genetics is promulgated as offering the most promising cure for disease: that is, gene therapy is marketed as having personal benefits for the individual and for potential offspring. It has been argued that this benefit is not always clear, since most diseases of the modern world are not genetic in a way that invites simple therapies. Nevertheless it is legitimated in terms of population benefits: the old concept of the magic bullet resurrected. The more simplistic idea that there is a quick fix associated with defective genes reinforces the definition of health and illness as related to individual characteristics rather than the social environment. In a sense this is the concept of health turning back to itself. Holistic medicine embraced a model of the healthy individual as a social whole, but here the body is being atomized down to its smallest components – which, in the end, represent its personal genetic uniqueness.

Conclusion

This discussion of the meaning of 'health' began with some simple definitions expressed in lay accounts, and concludes with speculations about the difficulties created for lay people by the technological and other changes in the modern world. Throughout history, health has always been a slightly slippery concept, with, as chapter 1 discussed, a variety of meanings. No single definition has been offered here, for the theme of the book has been not only that a single all-purpose definition of health is impossible, but that attempts to impose one have never been very functional.

One of the most pervasive ideas has always been some concept of normality, though what is normal is obviously historically specific, culturally defined, and dependent on the state of knowledge at the time. Health has commonly been defined in functional terms, as the efficiency of bodily systems and fitness for the tasks that people want to perform, as balance or homeostasis, as psychosocial feelings of well-being or happiness, or for more than a century in Western societies as not diseased, injured, or otherwise malfunctioning according to a 'medical model' associated with the science and profession of medicine. Consideration of the way that the concept has changed throughout history and has developed in different cultures demonstrates its shifting nature, and the now extensive body of research on lay formulations and beliefs shows how clearly these are patterned not only by history but also by characteristics such as age and gender and the circumstances of people's lives. An important point which has been made is that neither in lay perceptions, nor as manifested in their actual experience, are health and illness simply logical opposites.

These ideas are important to those who try to cure disease, and to those who influence the policy of health services. People's actions, including their help-seeking behaviour, how they act when they are ill, and their health-harming or health-protecting lifestyles, are all affected by the way in which they perceive that disease is caused and health is manifested. Chapter 4 began to introduce questions of structure and agency with regard to health, or the extent to which health is determined by forces outside the individual's control or, alternatively, is in their own hands.

Questions were also raised about the extent to which health is nowadays defined by the governments who exercise surveillance over it and by the commercial interests who turn it into a commodity. Chapter 5 turned more explicitly to health as a social and political issue, and the way in which individual experience may be the product of a society's resources and the way they are organized. Explanations have to be sought for the differences between countries in general levels of health, and between groups within countries. The perception and definition of health inequalities, and particularly the study of their causes, leads to new theories of what health is and how it is determined. Here, ideas about the 'socio-biologic translation' by which stresses are thought to become manifest in disease, the concept of 'social capital', and newer critiques of this neo-liberal position were introduced.

Finally, chapter 6 considered the place of health in the 'risk society' and its definition in postmodern societies undergoing flux and change. The blurring of the clear distinctions between ill and not-ill, self and not-self, life and not-life all require new ethical considerations. In previous eras, it is difficult to think of scientific discoveries and technological breakthroughs in the field of health where the ethical questions is not 'how can we afford, or how should we distribute, the fruits of this life-saving or enhancing advance?', but 'is it ethical to make use of this new knowledge?' Any definition of disease as deviation from the normal, with the purpose of medical therapy as the restoration of normality, is unsettled: many new technologies offer the possibility of *enhancing* the normal. At the same time as consumerist society puts ever greater emphasis on medicine and what it can achieve, the idea of health as a universally prior value is questioned. Defined simply as the absence of disease or illness it is – as lay accounts have always declared – not the only or uncomplicated goal of life.

One theme throughout has been that health is (in people's perceptions, as well as logically) a positive state, different from the simple absence of illness or disease. But this positive concept becomes ever more complex and difficult to define. More and more, it appears to be an interaction between people and their environment. This resonates with the experience of health as both inside and outside the self, but how it affects the apparently fundamental perception of the *moral* nature of health is not yet clear: all that is obvious is that there are new moral issues.

The theme of choice and responsibility has been pervasive throughout this volume, in relation to health policy and also to the way in which health is perceived. The emphasis of self-determination and the enhancement of freedom of choice in the discussion of the new genetics again reflects an increasing emphasis on active citizenship in Western societies. Policy turns particularly to creating conditions that allow and enable self-government. However, at the same time genetics individualizes, placing ill health firmly within rather than without, but also removing active responsibility. How individuals struggle with this dilemma is not very well understood. There is in fact some argument that the mere availability of new technologies creates pressures for their use, and some concern that they may allow governments, commercial interests and the scientific community to market their own objectives under the banner of therapy and consumer choice.

It is hardly original to note that the pace of change is accelerating, but it is perhaps important to point to the variety of forces driving change, and that the resultant ambiguities between life and the inanimate, the individual and public health, mind and body, require continual monitoring. Meanwhile, the ill person is where he or she always was – trying to find a moral identity, trying to live in an uncertain and unreliable body, and trying to make the most of their allotted time in a changing world.

References

Antonovsky, A. 1979: *Health, Stress and Coping*. San Francisco: Jossey-Bass.

Arksey, H. 1994: Expert and lay participation in the construction of medical knowledge. *Sociology of Health & Illness*, 16, 448–68.

Armstrong, D. 1993: From clinical gaze to regime of total health. In A. Beattie, M. Gott, L. Jones and M. Sidell (eds) *Health and Wellbeing*. London: Macmillan and Open University, 55–67.

Armstrong, D. 1995: The rise of surveillance medicine. *Sociology of Health & Illness*, 17, 397–404.

Baudrillard, J. 1983: *Simulations*. New York: Semiotext.

Bauman, B. 1961: Diversities in conceptions of health and physical fitness. *Journal of Health and Human Behaviour*, 2, 39–47.

Beck, U. 1992: *Risk Society: Towards a New Modernity*. London: Sage.

Becker, H. S. 1963: *Outsiders: Studies in the Sociology of Deviance*. New York: Free Press.

Blair, A. 1993: Social class and the contextualization of illness experience. In A. Radley (ed.) *Worlds of Illness: Biographical and Cultural Perspectives on Health and Disease*. London: Routledge, 27–48.

Blaxter, M. 1978: Diagnosis as category and process: the case of alcoholism. *Social Science & Medicine*, 12 (1), 9–17.

Blaxter, M. 1983: The causes of disease: women talking. *Social Science & Medicine*, 1 (2), 59–69.

Blaxter, M. 1990: *Health and Lifestyles*. London: Routledge.

Blaxter, M. 1993: Why do the victims blame themselves? In A. Radley (ed.) *Worlds of Illness: Biographical and Cultural Perspectives on Health and Disease*. London: Routledge, 124–42.

Blaxter, M. 2000: Class, time and biography. In S. J. Williams, J. Gabe and M. Calnan (eds) *Health, Medicine and Society: Key Theories, Future Agendas*. London: Routledge, 27–50.

Blaxter, M. 2002: *Social Capital and Definitions of Health*. Social Capital WP3, University of East Anglia.

Blaxter, M., and Paterson, E. 1982: *Mothers and Daughters: A Three-Generational Study of Health Attitudes and Behaviour*. London: Heinemann.

Blumer, H. 1969: *Symbolic Interactionism*. Englewood Cliffs, NJ: Prentice-Hall.

Bobak, M., Pikhart, H., Rose, R., Hertzman, C., and Marmot, M. 2000: Socioeconomic factors, material inequalities, and perceived control in self-rated health: cross-sectional data from seven post-communist countries. *Social Science & Medicine*, 51, 1343–50.

Bourdieu, P. 1984: *Distinction: A Social Critique of the Judgement of Taste*. London: Routledge.

Bunton, R., and Burrows, R. 1995: Consumption and health in the 'epidemiological' clinic of late modern medicine. In R. Bunton, S. Nettleton and R. Burrows (eds) *The Sociology of Health Promotion*. London: Routledge, 206–22.

Bury, M. 2001: Illness narratives: fact or fiction? *Sociology of Health & Illness*, 23, 263–85.

Calnan, M. 1987: *Health and Illness: The Lay Perspective*. London: Tavistock.

Chisholm, J. 1998: Evolutionary medicine. In A. Petersen and C. Waddell (eds) *Health Matters*. Buckingham: Open University Press, 72–87.

Chrysanthou, M. 2002: Transparency and selfhood: Utopia and the informed body. *Social Science & Medicine*, 54, 469–79.

Coburn, D. 2000: Income inequality, social cohesion and the health status of populations: the role of neo-liberalism. *Social Science & Medicine*, 51, 135–46.

Coleman, J. S. 1988: Social capital in the creation of human capital. *American Journal of Sociology*, S95–120.

Conrad, P. 1999: A mirage of genes. *Sociology of Health & Illness*, 21, 228–41.

Cornwell, J. 1984: *Hard-Earned Lives: Accounts of Health and Illness from East London*. London: Tavistock.

Cox, B., Huppert, F. A., and Wichelow, M. 1993: *The Health and Lifestyle Survey: Seven Years On*. Aldershot: Dartmouth.

Cox, S., and McKellin, W. 1999: 'There's this thing in our family': predictive testing and the construction of risk for Huntington's Disease. *Sociology of Health & Illness*, 21, 622–46.

Crawford, R. 1977: You are dangerous to your health: the ideology and politics of victim blaming. *International Journal of Health Services*, 7, 663–78.

Crawford, R. 1984: A cultural account of 'health': control, release and the social body. In J. B. McKinlay (ed.) *Issues in the Political Economy of Health Care*. London: Tavistock; abridged in A. Beattie, M. Gott, L. Jones and M. Sidell (1993) (eds) *Health and Wellbeing*. London: Macmillan Press and Open University, 133–43.

Crawford, R. 2000: The ritual of health promotion. In S. J. Williams, J. Gabe and M. Calnan (eds) *Health, Medicine and Society: Key Theories, Future Agendas*. London: Routledge, 219–35.

Davey Smith, G., Gunnel, D. C., and Ben-Shlomo, Y. 2001: Life-course approaches to socio-economic differentials in cause-specific adult mortality. In D. Leon and G. Walt (eds) *Poverty, Inequality and Health*. Oxford: Oxford University Press, 88–124.

Davison, C., Davey Smith, G., and Frankel, S. 1991: Lay epidemiology and the prevention paradox: the implications of coronary candidacy for health education. *Sociology of Health & Illness*, 13 (1), 1–19.

Department of Health and Social Services 1980: *Inequalities in Health* (Black Report). London: DHSS.

Derrida, J. 1982: *Margins of Philosophy*. Hemel Hempstead: Harvester.

D'Houtard, A., and Field, M. 1986: New research on the image of health. In C. Currer and M. Stacey (eds) *Concepts of Health, Illness and Disease*. Leamington Spa: Berg.

Dickens, P. 2000: *Social Darwinism*. Milton Keynes: Open University Press.

Douglas, M. 1970: *Natural Symbols: Essays in Anthropology*. London: Routledge & Kegan Paul.

Douglas, M. 1992: *Risk and Blame*. London: Routledge.

Douglas, M., and Wildavsky, A. 1982: *Risk and Culture: An Essay on the Selection of Technical and Environmental Dangers*. Berkeley: University of California Press.

Dubos, R. J. 1959: *Mirage of Health*. New York: Harper.

Dubos, R. J. 1965: *Man Adapting*. New Haven, CT: Yale University Press.

Ehrenreich, A., and English, D. 1978: The 'sick' women of the upper classes. In J. Ehrenreich (ed.) *The Cultural Crisis of Modern Medicine*. New York: Monthly Review Press.

Elliott, A. 2001: *Concepts of the Self*. Cambridge: Polity.
Engel, R. L. 1963: Medical diagnosis: present, past and future. *Archives of Internal Medicine*, 112, 520–9.
Erde, E. 1979: Philosophical considerations regarding defining 'health', 'disease', etc. and their bearing on medical practice. *Ethics in Science & Medicine*, 6, 31–48.
Fabrega, H. 1976a: The biological significance of taxonomies of disease. *Journal of Theoretical Biology*, 63, 191–216.
Fabrega, H. 1976b: Toward a theory of human disease. *Journal of Nervous and Mental Diseases*, 162, 299–312.
Fabrega, H. 1977: The scope of ethnomethodological science. *Culture Medicine & Psychiatry*, 1, 201–28.
Fleck, L. [1935] 1979: *Genesis and Development of a Scientific Fact*. Chicago: University of Chicago Press.
Foley, M. W., and Edwards, B. 1999: Is it time to disinvest in social capital? *Journal of Public Policy*, 19, 141–73.
Foucault, M. 1973: *The Birth of the Clinic*. London: Tavistock.
Foucault, M. 1977: *Discipline and Punish: The Birth of the Prison*. London: Allen Lane.
Frank, A. W. 1991: *At the Will of the Body: Reflection on Illness*. Boston: Houghton-Mifflin.
Frank, A. 1992: Twin nightmares of the medical simulacrum. In W. Stearns and W. Chaloupke (eds) *Jean Baudrillard: The Disappearance of Art and Politics*. London: Macmillan, 82–97.
Frank, A. 1995: *The Wounded Storyteller: Body, Illness and Ethics*. Chicago and London: University of Chicago Press.
Frankenberg, R. 1992: Your time or mine: temporal contradictions of biomedical practice. In R. Frankenberg (ed.) *Time, Health and Medicine*. London: Sage, 1–30.
Freidson, E. 1960: Client control and medical practice. *American Journal of Sociology*, 65, 374–82.
Freidson, E. 1965: Disability as social deviance. In M. B. Sussman (ed.) *Sociology of Disability and Rehabilitation*. Washington, DC: American Sociological Association.
Giddens, A. 1991: *Modernity and Self-Identity: Self and Society in the Late Modern Age*. Cambridge: Polity.
Glasner, B. 1995: In the name of health. In R. Bunton, S. Nettleton and R. Burrows (eds) *The Sociology of Health Promotion*. London: Routledge, 159–75.
Goffman, E. 1967: *Stigma: Notes on the Management of Spoiled Identity*. Englewood Cliffs, NJ: Prentice-Hall.
Good, B. J. 1994: *Medicine, Rationality and Experience: An Anthropological Perspective*. Cambridge: Cambridge University Press.

Hallowell, N. 1999: Doing the right thing: genetic risk and responsibility. *Sociology of Health & Illness*, 21, 597–621.

Hallowell, N., and Lawton, J. 2002: Negotiating present and future selves: managing the risk of hereditary ovarian cancer by prophylatic surgery. *Health*, 6, 423–43.

Hardey, M. 1999: Doctor in the house: the Internet as a source of lay health knowledge and the challenge to expertise. *Sociology of Health & Illness*, 21, 820–35.

Harley, D. 1999: Rhetoric and the social construction of sickness and healing. *Social History of Medicine*, 12, 408–35.

Helman, C. 1978: Feed a cold, starve a fever. *Culture Medicine & Psychiatry*, 2, 107–37.

Herzlich, C. 1973: *Health and Illness*. London: Academic Press.

Herzlich, C., and Pierret, J. 1985: The social construction of the patient: patients and illnesses in other ages. *Social Science & Medicine*, 20, 145–51.

Herzlich, C., and Pierret, J. 1987: *Illness and Self in Society*. Baltimore: John Hopkins University Press.

Hippocrates 1993: *Aphorisms*, trans. W. H. S. Jones. London and Cambridge, MA: Heinemann/Harvard University Press.

Hyden, L. C. 1997: Illness and narrative. *Sociology of Health & Illness*, 19, 48–69.

Illich, I. 1974: Medical nemesis. *The Lancet*, 11 May, 918–22.

Jewson, N. D. 1976: The disappearance of the sick man from medical cosmology 1770–1870. *Sociology*, 10, 225–44.

Kendall, R. E. 1975: The concept of disease and its implications for psychiatry. *British Journal of Psychiatry*, 127, 305–15.

Kenen, R. 1994: The human genome project: creator of the potentially sick, potentially vulnerable and potentially stigmatized? In I. Robinson (ed.) *The Social Consequences of Life and Death under High Technology Medicine*. Manchester: Manchester University Press.

Kenen, R. 1996: The at-risk health status and technology: a diagnostic invitation and the 'gift' of knowing. *Social Science & Medicine*, 42, 1545–53.

Kleinman, A. 1980: *Patients and Healers in the Context of Culture: An Exploration of the Borderland between Anthropology, Medicine and Psychiatry*. Berkeley and London: University of California Press.

Koos, E. 1954: *The Health of Regionville: What the People Thought and Did About it*. New York: Columbia University Press.

Kunitz, S. J. 2001: Accounts of social capital: the mixed health effects of personal communities and voluntary groups. In D. Leon and G. Walt (eds) *Poverty, Inequality & Health*. Oxford: Oxford University Press, 159–74.

Kunst, A. E., Groenhof, F., Mackenbach, J. P., et al. 1998: Mortality by occupational class among men 30–64 years in 11 European countries. *Social Science & Medicine*, 46, 1459–76.

Lahelma, E., Kivela, K., Roos E., et al. 2002: Analysing changes of health inequalities in the Nordic welfare states. *Social Science & Medicine*, 55, 609–25.

Linder, R. 1965: Diagnosis: description or prescription? A case study in the psychology of diagnosis. *Perceptual & Motor Skills*, 20, 1081–92.

Lock, M. 2002: *Twice Dead: Organ Transplants and the Reinvention of Death*. Berkeley and Los Angeles: University of California Press.

Lupton, D. 1995: *The Imperative of Health: Public Health and the Regulated Body*. London: Sage.

Macintyre, S. 1997: The Black Report and beyond: what are the issues? *Social Science & Medicine*, 44, 723–45.

McKee, M. 2001: The health consequences of the collapse of the Soviet Union. In D. Leon and G. Walt (eds) *Poverty, Inequality & Health*. Oxford: Oxford University Press, 17–36.

McKeown, T. 1976: *The Role of Medicine: Dream, Mirage or Nemesis?* London: Nuffield Provincial Hospitals Trust.

McKeown, T., Record, R. G., and Turner, R. D. 1975: An interpretation of the decline in mortality in England and Wales during the twentieth century. *Population Studies*, 29, 391–422.

Marmot, M. G., and Feeney, A. 1996: Work and health: implications for individuals and society. In D. Blane, E. Brunner and R. Wilkinson (eds) *Health and Social Organisation*. London: Routledge.

Marmot, M. G., Shipley, M. J., and Rose, G. 1984: Inequalities in death-specific explanations of a general pattern. *The Lancet*, i, 1003–6.

Martin, E. 2000: Flexible bodies: science and a new culture of health in the US. In S. J. Williams, J. Gabe and M. Calnan (eds) *Health, Medicine & Society: Key Theories, Future Agendas*. London: Routledge, 123–45.

May, C., Gask, L., Atkinson, T., Ellis, N., and Mair, F. 2001: Resisting and promoting new technologies in clinical practice: the case of telepsychiatry. *Social Science & Medicine*, 52, 1889–901.

Mead, G. H. 1934: *Mind, Self and Society*. Chicago: University of Chicago Press.

Mechanic, D. 1968: *Medical Sociology*. New York: Free Press.

Mechanic, D. 2002: Socio-cultural implications of changing organizational technologies in the provision of care. *Social Science & Medicine*, 54, 459–67.

Michie, S., McDonald, V., and Marteau, T. 1996: Understanding responses to predictive genetic testing: a grounded theory approach. *Psychology and Health*, 11, 455–70.

Mishler, E. G. 1981: Critical perspectives on the biomedical model, and the social construction of illness. In E. G. Mishler, L. A. Aramasingham, S. T. Hanser, R. Liem, S. D. Osherson and N. E. Waxler (eds) *Social Contexts of Health, Illness, and Patient Care*. Cambridge: Cambridge University Press, 1–23 and 141–68.

Muntaner, C., Lynch, J., and Davey Smith, G. 2000: Social capital and the third way in public health. *Critical Public Health*, 10, 107–24.

Navarro, V. 1976: *Medicine under Capitalism*. London: Croom Helm.

Nelkin, D., and Andrews, L. 1999: DNA identification and surveillance creep. *Sociology of Health & Illness*, 21, 689–706.

Neve, M. 1995: Ch. 8. In L. I. Conrad, M. Neve, V. Nutton, R. Porter and A. Wear (eds) *The Western Medical Tradition 800BC to AD1800*. Cambridge: Cambridge University Press, 477–94.

Nicolson, M., and McLaughlin, C. 1988: Social constructionism and medical sociology: a study of the vascular theory of multiple sclerosis. *Sociology of Health & Illness*, 10, 234–61.

Oakley, A. 1976: Wisewomen and Medicineman: changes in the management of childbirth. In J. Mitchell and A. Oakley (eds) *The Rights and Wrongs of Women*. Harmondsworth: Penguin.

Parsons, T. 1951: *The Social System*. New York: Free Press.

Pierret, J. 1993: Constructing discourses about health and their social determinants. In A. Radley (ed.) *Worlds of Illness: Biographical and Cultural Perspectives on Health and Disease*. London: Routledge, 9–26.

Pill, R., and Stott, N. 1982: Concepts of illness causation and responsibility. *Social Science & Medicine*, 16, 43–52.

Pill, R., and Stott, N. 1987: Development of a measure of potential health behaviour: a salience of lifestyle index. *Social Science & Medicine*, 24, 125–34.

Pollock, K. 1993: Attitude of mind as a means of resisting illness. In A. Radley (ed.) *Worlds of Illness: Biographical and Cultural Perspectives on Health and Disease*. London: Routledge, 49–70.

Porn, J. 1993: Health and adaptedness. *Theoretical Medicine*, 14, 295–303.

Posner, T. 1977: Magical elements in orthodox medicine: diabetes as a medical thought system. In R. Dingwall, C. Heath, M. Reid and M. Stacey (eds) *Health Care and Health Knowledge*. London: Croom Helm, 142–58.

Prior, L. 2000: Reflection on the 'mortal' body in late modernity. In S. J. Williams, J. Gabe and M. Calnan (eds) *Health, Medicine and Society: Key Theories, Future Agendas*. London: Routledge, 186–202.

Prior, L., Wood, F., Gray, J., Pill, R., and Hughes, D. 2002: Making risk visible: the role of images in the assessment of (cancer) genetic risk. *Health Risk and Society*, 4, 241–58.

Putnam, R. D. 1995: Bowling alone: America's declining social capital. *Journal of Democracy*, 6, 65–78.

Quah, S. 2001: Health and culture. In W. C. Cockerham (ed.) *The Blackwell Companion to Medical Sociology*. Oxford: Blackwell, 23–42.

Radley, A., and Billig, M. 1996: Accounts of health and illness: dilemmas and representations. *Sociology of Health & Illness*, 18, 220–40.

Radley, A., and Green, R. 1987: Illness and adjustment. *Sociology of Health & Illness*, 9, 179–207.

Richards, M. P. M. 1993: The new genetics: some issues for social scientists. *Sociology of Health & Illness*, 15, 567–86.

Robinson, D. 1971: *The Process of Becoming Ill*. London: Routledge & Kegan Paul.

Rosenstock, I. M. 1974: Historical origins of the health belief model. *Health Education Monographs*, 2, 328–35.

Sanner, M. A. 2001: Exchanging spare parts or becoming a new person? People's attitudes toward receiving and donating organs. *Social Science & Medicine*, 52, 1491–9.

Scheff, T. J. 1966: *Being Mentally Ill: A Sociological Theory*. Chicago: Aldine.

Scott, R. A. 1966: The selection of clients by social welfare agencies: the case of the blind. *Social Problems*, 14.

Scott, W. J. 1990: PTSD in DSM-III: a case in the politics of diagnosis and disease. *Social Problems*, 37, 294–310.

Seale, C. 2000: Changing patterns of death and dying. *Social Science & Medicine*, 51, 917–30.

Seale, C., and Pattison, S. (eds) 1994: *Medical Knowledge: Doubt and Certainty*. Buckingham: Open University Press.

Sedgwick, P. 1973: Illness, mental and otherwise. *Hastings Center Studies*, 1, 19–40.

Sharp, L. A. 1995: Organ transplantations as a transformative experience: anthropological insights into the restructuring of the self. *Medical Anthropology Quarterly*, 9, 357–89.

Sontag, S. 1979: *Illness as Metaphor*. New York: Vintage.

Stainton Rogers, W. 1991: *Explaining Health and Illness*. London: Harvester Wheatsheaf.

Swann, C., and Morgan, A. (eds) 2002: *Social Capital for Health: Insights from Qualitative Research*. London: Health Development Agency.

Szasz, T. S. 1961: *The Myth of Mental Illness*. London: Secker & Warburg.

Tarlov, A. R. 1996: Social determinants of health: the sociobiological translation. In D. Blane, E. Brunner and R. Wilkinson (eds) *Health and Social Organisation*. London: Routledge.

Turner, B. S. 1984: *Regulating Bodies*. London: Routledge.

Turner, B. S. 1996: *The Body and Society*. London: Sage.

Wadsworth, M. E. J. 1991: *The Imprint of Time*. Oxford: Clarendon Press.

Waldby, C. 1998: Medical imaging: the biopolitics of visibility. *Health*, 2, 372–84.

Waldby, C. 2002: Stem cells, tissue cultures and the production of biovalue. *Health*, 6, 305–23.

Wertz, D. C. 1992: Ethical and legal implications of the new genetics. *Social Science & Medicine*, 35, 495–505.

Whitehead, M. 1990: *The Concepts and Principles of Equity and Health*. Copenhagen: WHO Regional Office for Europe.

Wilkinson, R. 1996: *Unhealthy Societies: The Afflictions of Inequality*. London: Routledge.

Wilkinson, R. 2000: *Mind the Gap: Hierarchies, Health and Human Evolution*. London: Weidenfeld & Nicolson.

Williams, G. 1984: The genesis of chronic illness: narrative reconstruction. *Sociology of Health & Illness*, 6, 175–200.

Williams, G. 1993: Chronic illness and the pursuit of virtue in everyday life. In A. Radley (ed.) *Worlds of Illness: Biographical and Cultural Perspectives on Health and Disease*. London: Routledge, 92–108.

Williams, G., and Busby, H. 2000: The politics of 'disabled' bodies. In S. J. Williams, J. Gabe and M. Calnan (eds) *Health, Medicine and Society: Key Theories, Future Agendas*. London: Routledge, 169–85.

Williams, R. 1990: *A Protestant Legacy*. Oxford: Clarendon Press.

Williams, S. J. 1996: The vicissitudes of embodiment across the chronic illness trajectory. *Body and Society*, 2, 23–47.

Williams, S. J. 1997: Modern medicine and the 'uncertain body': from corporeality to hyperreality? *Social Science & Medicine*, 45, 1041–9.

Williams, S. J., and Bendelow, G. 1998: *The Lived Body: Sociological Themes, Embodied Issues*. London: Routledge.

World Health Organization, Regional Office for Europe, 1998: *Health 21: Health for All in the 21st Century*. Copenhagen: WHO.

Wyatt, J. C. 1996: Commentary: telemedicine trials – clinical pull or technology push? *MB Journal*, 313, 1380–1.

Zola, I. K. 1973: Pathways to the doctor – from person to patient. *Social Science & Medicine*, 7, 677–89.

Zola, I. K. 1975: Medicine as an institution of social control. In C. Cox and A. Mead (eds) *A Sociology of Medical Practice*. New York: Macmillan, 170–88.

Index